Self Defense Solutions

By

Neal Martin

Copyright © 2014 Neal Martin

All rights reserved.

This book or any portion thereof may not be reproduced or used in any manner whatsoever without the express written permission of the publisher except for the use of brief quotations in a book review.

Table of Contents

Introduction 1

Chapter 1 | Target Hardening 5

Chapter 2 | Some Truths about Combatives 17

Chapter 3 | Pad Drill Training 29

Chapter 4 | Improving Your Striking 38

Chapter 5 | Intent 52

Chapter 6 | Support Skills for Better Offence and Defence 60

Chapter 7 | Three Major Flaws in Combatives Training and How to Fix Them 67

Chapter 8 | Bad Training Habits 78

Chapter 9 | Live Fight Training and Developing Fighting Instincts 87

Chapter 10 | Reality Dyslexia 93

Chapter 11 | Vital Attack Points 103

Chapter 12 | Create Space or Close Distance? 109

Chapter 13 | Force Disparity and Control and Restraint 119

Chapter 14 | Self Defence Psychology And Mental Training 128

Chapter 15 | Taking Your Time 141

Afterward	151
Other Books By Neal Martin	154
About The Author	158

Dedication

To B

Acknowledgments

I would like to thank everyone who continues to train with me and support me, especially all at On Guard and those who continue to follow me on Combative Mind. Once again, thanks to Mick Coup for his continued inspiration and helping me stay on the right path. Finally thanks to my wife and all of my family for their continued support.

Neal Martin

Introduction

If you have read my other books then you know I don't write conventional self-defence books. This book is no different.

If you are looking for a picture book with lots of different techniques nicely laid out then you might as well stop reading now and go pick up that five hundred page Krav Maga book instead. I don't see the point in those kinds of books, simply because they imply that you can learn self-defence from a book.

You can't learn self-defence from a book. To learn self-defence you have to train under a credible instructor. That's all there is to it.

I'm assuming you know that already though. I'm also assuming that you currently train on a regular basis with actual people and that you aren't one of these deluded souls who think staring at a bunch of photo sequences will make them into awesome fighters.

This is a book for serious combatives practitioners, for those who train on a regular basis and who want to improve their skills. It's also for those who don't shy away from a little thinking and who don't mind working some things out for themselves.

I've written this book for those who would like to change and improve their approach to training (and self defence in general). How you approach your training can make all the difference. If you approach things the wrong way then you will not get the results that you are looking for. So this is a book that will help you refine your approach to certain aspects of training so you can hopefully improve upon the results you are currently getting.

Read through the book and take out of it what is useful to you. The information you are about to read is a representation of my own approach to self-defence and combatives training. It's an approach that has taken a lot of learning (on my own and under other instructors in the field) and a lot of hard work to formulate.

This book is not representative of all aspects of combatives or self defence, but I have included what I think will be most useful to you—stuff that will have a broad effect on your overall training and attitude to training.

This isn't a technical how-to book either, but you will find many practical tips in these pages. You will also find things in it that will hopefully trigger in you a desire to examine your own training and to possibly explore different options and ways of doing things that will end up improving upon the results you are getting at the moment.

I say that not to devalue the worth of your current training. I don't know what it is you do, but with everyone, there is always room for improvement.

Study the information in this book, but also be sure to apply it in your own training. That is the only way you will know if there is any practical value in the information I am offering here.

Test things out, don't just read about them.

There is always more to learn and discover. My hope is that this book will help you in that regard. I don't have all the answers (does anyone?) but I can certainly point you in the right direction.

There is no particular order to the chapters in this book. Realistically, you could start reading whichever chapter you want first, for they are all stand- alone. At the same time, each chapter is a piece of a bigger theme—that theme being how to improve the results you are getting from your training by altering your approach to certain aspects of it.

Strive for truth and honesty in your training and you won't go far wrong.

Neal Martin

Chapter 1|Target Hardening

Before we get to talking about combatives training and the physical side of self-defence, I thought it a good idea to spend this first chapter of the book talking about target hardening. In other words, how to protect oneself against unwanted attention and violence in the first place.

Even though I have talked about this aspect of self-defence at length in my first book, I feel this information bears repeating. Your goal, when it comes to self-protection, should be to avoid any kind of trouble in the first place by implementing awareness and avoidance strategies into your gameplan. So in this chapter I will discuss some of the ways in which you can do that. We will start with a website called Quora.

Quora is a bit like Yahoo Answers in that people ask questions on a whole range of different subjects and other people give their answers to those questions. One of the categories in Quora is self-defence, which I like to check out now and again just to see what people are talking about. During one of my visits to the site I came across this question:

"What is the best form of self-defence for a woman who is very small (shorter than 5'3)?"

A friend of mine has confided in me that she is not just cat-called on the streets, but that creepy older guys have actually walked up behind her and whispered sexual things in her ears, and guys have even driven up to her on motorcycles and groped her before driving off.

What could she do to protect herself in these situations? Scream loudly? Carry a knife? Taser? Pepper-spray? Learn martial arts?

A few people answered this question, but by far the best answer was this one, from a woman called Bianca, who is a nurse:

"The first and best self-defense weapon for a small woman is your voice. PERIOD.

"I'm not even 5 foot tall and have worked in a dangerous field for almost 20 years. I've worked in a forensic psychiatric hospital and now work in a drug rehab. All men, usually. The psych hospital housed murderers, rapists, child molesters, etc.

Neal Martin

"We were trained in self-defense, yes, but my voice is what saved me from injury far more than any self-defense classes would.

"People don't want a lot of noise when they're committing a crime and YES, men driving up and fondling you IS A CRIME.

"YELL. If a creepy old man is walking behind you, especially if he's close enough to WHISPER IN YOUR EAR, YELL!

"GET AWAY FROM ME! I DON'T KNOW YOU!"

"Calling attention to the situation will generally make that person get away from you. They don't want to go to jail. They don't want others to notice what they're doing.

"Aside from that, keep your phone with you at all times. Call 911. Call the authorities.

"The situations you've described are UNACCEPTABLE! I'm not placing blame on your friend but WHERE IS SHE HANGING OUT WHERE THESE THINGS ARE HAPPENING THIS FREQUENTLY?

"She needs to walk with confidence. Show no fear. Men don't DO things like that to me and I'm not disgusting or anything. I think they just know better. I walk with confidence. Perhaps even an ATTITUDE.

"I can hear it now, "That little thing just THINKS she's safe" but I've spent YEARS swimming with sharks. How you carry yourself speaks volumes to criminals.

"If it makes you feel better, carry some pepper spray. Take some self-defense courses. A knife is a bad idea, in my opinion. You have to be pretty close to someone to use a knife and they don't do the damage you really hope for in a struggle. You might not even get to use it. Perhaps the perp will even take it from you.

"All I carry with me is a HUGE voice, an awareness of my surroundings, and an attitude problem. It's served me well."

Great answer, right? It highlighted a few problems that people often have when it comes to self-defence, such as a lack of awareness and no situational control skills.

But the issue brought up here that I am most interested in is how you put yourself across to other people, and especially those people who you really don't want anywhere near you, such as the undesirables described in the Quora question.

Neal Martin

Target Hardening

Target hardening, the concept of making oneself a hard target for criminals by fortifying yourself against their advances, is massively important. If you have no defences in place that will repel those who would seek to take advantage then you are just a walking open invitation to anyone who feels like messing with you. In other words, you will exhibit a *victim profile*, just like the woman described in the Quora question.

How you carry yourself and how you interact with other people speaks volumes about the kind of person you are. Those who have made it their business to seek out and victimize other people know just what to look for in a potential target victim. They know the profile: lack of confidence in the way someone carries themselves; lack of assertiveness; overly polite and willing to let strangers into their personal space; easily controlled and manipulated—the exact opposite of a hard target.

I discovered a long time ago that the way you carry yourself in public has a massive bearing on how other people treat you. If you carry yourself with confidence, in general you will attract less trouble.

In my experience, the quieter that confidence is the better. Cockiness and arrogance can still attract trouble.

I've always found that people are more respectful of someone who is quietly confident and not too overbearing.

A quiet confidence comes from having the attitude that you have nothing to prove. Arrogant and over-confident people quite often come across like they have something to prove, and usually there will be someone there who will challenge them on that. I don't know about you, but I don't need that kind of attention. I like to be left alone when I'm out and about.

Having a quiet confidence will still communicate to have-a-go dickheads that you are not an easy target, without having to broadcast this fact every chance you get and risk aggravating the wrong person or persons.

I've been out before with some very extroverted people who didn't know how to keep their mouths shut. They would challenge anyone at the drop of a hat. Inevitably they would end up scrapping with someone. One night a friend and I found ourselves being chased by a gang of twenty lads over the head of such a person (that was a fun experience, especially once they surrounded us!).

You don't need to be an asshole to protect yourself. In fact, being an asshole will have the opposite effect and will attract trouble *to* you.

Be confident, be self-assured, but remain relaxed and try to keep your needy ego out of the equation.

Increasing Your Confidence

But how does one get this kind of confidence? How would the woman described in the Quora question get this kind of confidence?

That's not a particularly easy question to answer. Suggestions of self-defence lessons, carrying pepper spray or some other weapon are just one part of the equation. A number of other factors contribute to forming a real sense of confidence that can be felt by others.

Bianca, who answered the question above, is obviously a confident woman, but I'd say most of that confidence came from her job as a nurse and having to deal with all sorts of difficult people day in and day out. Time spent in that kind of environment will naturally increase anyone's confidence.

There is no quick fix for growing your confidence, despite what many self-help gurus will tell you.

To increase your confidence you have to put yourself in situations that demand confidence from you.

For many people, this means doing challenging jobs, dealing with problematic people or having to cope with difficult situations on a regular basis.

Working as a bouncer helped me grow my confidence when it came to dealing with difficult people and demanding situations. After a while I got used to it and found ways of being comfortable (or as comfortable as one can be) with such situations. This in turn gave me a sense of confidence that I could carry into other areas of my life.

In terms of making yourself a hard target, the starting point would have to be making that initial decision in your own mind that *you will never be anybody's victim.*

If a person is being victimised on a regular basis it is because, most of the time, they allow themselves to be victimized. They invite trouble upon themselves in some way. That may be a bit of a blanket statement, but if you think about it, it's true.

Whatever you have in your life you have invited it in in some way.

What signals is a person putting out that cause them to attract the people who do these acts? Why are they chosen over another?

In some way, they fit the victim profile.

You therefore make the decision to no longer come across as a victim.

Then what?

Then you begin to fortify yourself against any attacks on your person. You begin to practice assertiveness. And yes, assertiveness needs to be practiced if it doesn't come naturally to you.

Practice saying no to people, but not in an arrogant way, rather in a quietly confident way. People will soon begin to respect you a lot more. They will also realise that they can no longer treat you like a doormat because you simply won't stand for it.

At some point you must stand up for yourself or forever remain the victim.

Using Your Voice

Bianca drew attention to the fact that she used her voice a lot to project her confidence and authority. Your voice is a powerful tool when it comes to communicating your intentions. Not so much what you say, but *how you say it* matters most.

Self Defense Solutions

I read somewhere that 10% of conflicts are due to a difference of opinion and 90% are due to wrong tone of voice. That statistic serves to highlight the importance of how you use your voice in a conflict situation.

Exactly how you use your voice will depend on the situation. Different circumstances will demand different responses. If you're a woman being followed or accosted by some creep, using your voice loudly and with a commanding tone will work better than using your voice in a quiet, pleading manner.

Similarly, if you are a man who is facing another man who is trying to start an argument with you, using your voice in a calm and levelled manner will de-escalate things quicker than using your voice in a loud, arrogant or accusatory way.

Sometimes it is better not to use your voice at all, and to just listen. Other times, for your own protection, you have to make full use of your voice.

And let's not forget the accompanying body language, which must match the tone of your voice. If there is a mismatch you will give away your lack of congruity and confidence. To be truly assertive, everything about you has to communicate the fact that *you are* assertive. Without this congruent state your communication will not be as powerful or as effective as it should be. You may fail in your attempts at persuasion. If a threat is not convinced by your actions they will not stop what they are doing.

A threat has to be convinced in some way that you are not worth pursuing or the conflict will continue.

It can be difficult being assertive if you are not used to being so. But everything is difficult at first. And like everything else, it gets easier. Eventually it will just be a natural part of who you are.

Physical Self-Defence and Target Hardening

Self-defence only works if you have all that other stuff in place. Without that bedrock of confidence and assertiveness you will not be able to use physical self-defence in an effective manner. You will simply allow yourself to be bullied and manipulated to the point where self-defence is no longer any use to you. It will be too late to use your physical skills. The game will be long over.

Physical training will obviously contribute to your overall confidence and self-esteem, but it can't be relied upon to give you everything that you need to survive in the big bad world.

Not all self-defence situations call for physical responses anyway. Situations where someone is being more subtly attacked, as in the case of sexual harassment or verbal assault, demand a different kind of response, one that can only come from an innate sense of confidence, assertiveness and the belief that you will not be bullied or victimized by anyone.

Living a life that is relatively trouble free, one where you don't attract the unwanted attention of every dickhead you come into contact with, requires more than just a few (or even many) self-defence lessons or the purchase of pepper spray or even a gun. It's not as simple as that. People who do martial arts and self-defence still get bullied, they still get victimized and they still get beaten up on occasion, but that is mainly because they are lacking in the essential qualities that we just discussed—those of confidence, assertiveness and even social intelligence.

Physical self-defence training is only part of the solution when it comes to making oneself a hard target. The rest of the solution lies within you. It's up to you to bring that power out so that you can learn to use it.

Chapter 2|Some Truths about Combatives

One of the things I have observed about many of those who train in combatives is the tendency to feel superior when they compare themselves to those who train in other martial arts systems. I have been guilty of this myself at times. Combatives training, with its emphasis on "real fighting", tends to make its practitioners believe they are superior street fighters, or more physically capable than those who train in regular martial arts.

This is blatant nonsense of course. The vast majority of those who claim to train in RBSD systems are, in reality, no more capable than the average martial artist or sport fighter. Indeed in many cases, I'd say a lot of those who claim to be more capable in fighting terms *just aren't*. They are, in fact, *much less* capable than many of those who train in combat sports like MMA.

Obviously the individual in question has a lot to do with it, but in the main, MMA fighters—with their generally superior fighting skill and conditioning—would likely annihilate your average combatives practitioner in a fight.

This is why I get annoyed when combatives guys try to downplay MMA for self-defence, claiming it is only good for competition. Sure, MMA guys train for a different context, but fighting is fighting when it kicks off. A person who has fought against many fully resisting opponents in the cage (opponents who don't hold back and fight as hard as they possibly can) is bound to be more capable in a fight than some guy whose only experience of fighting is against a compliant partner in a padded suit who is barely trying.

The point I am trying to make here is that too many combatives practitioners view combatives training itself as infallible and beyond any kind of reproach. Combatives training can give a person a good advantage when it comes to self-defence, *but only if the training is right*. Even then, combatives training can still have its downsides which must be addressed if practitioners are to get the most from it.

So here, for the sake of balance, we will look at four downsides to combatives training and what can be done to address those downsides.

1. Combatives training can increase people's paranoia and feed their insecurities.

To my mind, one of the main benefits of combatives training is that it can greatly increase a person's confidence and self-esteem. I've observed this effect in many of the students I have trained over the years and it is great to see.

On the other hand, I've seen combatives training have the opposite effect on some people. I've seen some individuals get more paranoid and insecure the longer they continue to train.

Here's martial artist Matt Thornton concurring on this:

"One would think that by training in "street" orientated martial arts, or combatives that emphasize the self-defense aspects of martial arts, to the exclusion of what they deem to be "sports" training, that these types of individuals would gain more confidence, more peace, more happiness, and become more comfortable within themselves as their skills at 'self-defense' grew.

Unfortunately, it has been my experience that the opposite seems to be true. Individuals that come to strictly "street" oriented martial arts, that were already prone to feelings of inadequacy, shame, physiological fear, and paranoia, tend to have those qualities magnified by such training, rather than eased."

If a person is generally led in life by their ego and they suffer from insecurity and a degree of paranoia, then combatives training can exacerbate these traits. I've seen it happen quite a few times.

Combatives often attracts a certain type of individual, and these individuals can suffer from an excess of psychological fear. The training, with its focus on extreme violence and outward aggression, does nothing to alleviate this fear in the individual. It just makes it worse.

As the scholar Robert Thurman put it:

"Once we are prone to hate and rage, we project around us a field of paranoia and all people become our potential enemies. We feel destructive towards them, and we assume they feel destructive towards us."

Thus you have guys walking around thinking that everyone is out to get them. To combat this feeling of paranoia they often adopt a very aggressive persona that is quick to violence.

The fact is, some people just aren't ready for the type of training that combatives offers. These people are better off going into combat sports where they can learn some humility and get a handle on their insecurities.

Combatives training is not meant to make a person quick to violence. It is supposed to shape a person into one who is aware of themselves and their environment, one who has the confidence to try other methods of problem solving in a conflict situation before resorting to violence.

To quote Thurman again:

"When we become cool, we don't project enmity on others; we can observe them more objectively, and if they are in fact out to cause trouble, we can quickly act to avoid it."

Combatives training is just a tool at the end of the day, and in the right hands it can be a very effective tool. But just like a gun, in the wrong hands combatives can be dangerous, for the individual practicing and for those around them. It is up to instructors to make sure they are not creating a monster out of certain people.

2. Many so-called combatives systems are fantasy based nonsense.

The above statement may be a strong one but it is nonetheless true. Quite a lot of the combatives and modern reality based self-defence systems around today are based more on fantasy than on fact. Don't believe me? Take a quick browse through YouTube and look at some of the videos that people have put up in the name of "real" or "reality" self-defence. What becomes clear when you watch many of these videos is that the people in them have no grasp of the issues involved in self-defence, nor any understanding of what constitutes a proper self-defence technique.

So when I meet people and they tell me they "do combatives" I don't immediately think that this person must know what they are doing when it comes to training for self-defence. Instead, I reserve judgement until I see for myself what it is they do. There are so many bullshit systems out there with the combatives label attached that just saying you train in combatives isn't enough. That no more qualifies you in self-defence than saying you're a black belt qualifies you as a good martial artist.

The proof is in what you do, not what you say you do.

Neal Martin

For a combatives system to be worth a damn it has to be based on truth, not somebody's version of the truth. The techniques have to be based on sound physics and they must also have been tested repeatedly in the real world, not just once or twice. Just because you managed to pull off a jumping spin kick outside the pub one night doesn't mean that technique is now a valid self-defence technique that should be taught to everyone.

Many combatives systems also operate on the premise that problems should be made to fit solutions instead of the other way around. So you have these techniques being taught that are only good for a problem that has been made up in the gym. Thus we see silly attack scenarios that would never happen in the real world, just so the people training can use the awesome technique they made up for the imaginary attack!

In some of the more commercial combatives systems we also see a lot of fantasy based stuff like weapon disarm techniques and defences that are straight out of a Jason Bourne movie.

The truth about most "combatives" systems is that they are deeply flawed and only cater to the fantasies of those who train in them. Good combatives systems are few and far between. The systems that contain stuff that actually works a high percentage of the time are often considered boring or lacking in material, due to the fact that they are based around only a handful of techniques. Such criticisms, however, are based on ignorance and a wilful blindness to the truth. The kinds of people who propagate such ignorant nonsense are the kinds of people who pay good money to have their fantasies indulged on a regular basis (kind of like visiting a brothel twice a week), and are the reason why you can't trust a system just because it is labelled combatives.

3. Instinctive fighting skills are not worked enough—if at all—in many combatives systems.

Most combatives systems are based around two things: pad drills and scenario training. Both of these training methods are perfectly valid if done correctly, but in my experience neither of these training methods are enough on their own to make someone into a half-way decent fighter.

Pad drills are essential in combatives training. I'm in no way denying that. The best way to learn correct technique, body mechanics, power generation etc. is by utilising pad drills to isolate and work the different components that make up the fundamental combatives techniques. I'll be going into detail on pad training in a later chapter.

Scenario training can be useful if done correctly. Unfortunately, most scenario training in combatives involves the use of a padded suit and unrealistic scenarios and attack sequences.

What tends to be missing in many combatives systems is what falls in between these two training methods, and that is the development of instinctive fighting skills. By that, I mean developing the ability to think on your feet, to react spontaneously to the demands of the situation and to use the techniques that are most effective in response to whatever your opponent is doing.

To an extent, fighting instinct *can* be developed through pad drills, *if* the drills themselves are correctly designed. But in my experience, pad drills will only get you so far. Fighting with a live opponent is a different matter and it requires practice in that very situation, not through hitting pads.

In general, if a fight goes beyond a few seconds in length then it will turn into some kind of brawl. Most pad drills are designed to help a trainee practice finishing a fight in the first few seconds. The thinking goes, if you don't finish the fight in those first few seconds then you are doing something wrong. This may be so, but in reality some situations do develop into protracted brawls and if you are not used to tussling with an attacker in this way then you will likely freeze as you will not know how to handle it.

In a sense I am talking here about specialist fighting techniques, things like wrestling and grappling skills, takedowns and even boxing. When you go beyond the fundamental combatives techniques, these are the type of skills you'll be moving on to learning.

One way to practice these is to pad up and go for it with a partner. Slug it out or move in to wrestle and grapple, which more often than not happens anyway. Just knowing how to manipulate the other person, knowing how to handle someone at that range, is very useful. The only way to learn that is through live fighting. It's not like normal sparring exactly, because you are sticking to the fundamental techniques you have learned through pad drill training, but you can also utilise wrestling and grappling techniques to manipulate your opponent into a better position so you can strike them. I'll deal with this aspect in more detail later in the book.

Combatives shouldn't be all about pad drills and scenario training. Utilise the kind of live fighting I just talked about, even normal sparring as well. It all helps mould you into a better fighter.

4. The wrong mindset is often instilled in combatives.

The kind of "combative mindset" often instilled into trainees of combatives is the kind of mindset that means you go ape-shit on whatever threat is in front of you.

All threats are not the same however. To ramp up your aggression levels and go nuts on anyone who dares confront you is unwise, in my opinion. Not every situation you will find yourself in will demand the same response. Indeed in some cases, if you tap into your inner animal and beat the hell out of someone, perhaps going too far, you may find yourself in jail, which these days is a very real possibility.

Too many combatives instructors advocate the whole macho, kill-or-be-killed attitude when it comes to self-defence. There is a certain usefulness in cultivating such an attitude, as long as you temper it with a little common sense and self-restraint. Personally, I'm not a fan of such blind aggression. I prefer to take a more detached attitude to things.

In my previous book I talked about the professional mindset, which is a combative mindset based on detachment and cold, controlled aggression. Admittedly this is an ideal that is hard to reach sometimes, especially in situations where emotions are high. The closer you can get to this mindset, however, the more control you will have over yourself and the situation you are in.

Tapping into the inner animal, going ape-shit on your attacker is fine if your back is really against the wall and you have no other options. In my experience though, most of the situations the average person will find themselves in are not life or death and can be dealt with without recourse to too much violence.

You have to at least *try* to maintain control of yourself in these situations, for your sake as well as the other person's. Advocating a lack of control through unbridled aggression is not the way to go to achieve that, yet many combatives instructors and systems do just that.

So combatives training isn't perfect. It does have its downsides like everything else. The purpose of the rest of this book is to show you how you can minimize those downsides by taking the correct approach to your training. We will start in the next chapter by looking at pad training.

Chapter 3|Pad Drill Training

Pad drills are an integral part of combatives training. If you are training in a system that revolves for the most part around striking, then you need to be able to properly utilise pad drills in order to practice those strikes.

When I first started training in combatives, the pad drills that I used were fairly basic. They mainly involved striking the pad while it was held in a completely static position. This may be fine for initially learning the basics of a particular technique, but in terms of actual application and being able to use that technique in a more "alive" manner, your pad drills have to evolve to meet the demands of a real situation.

It wasn't until I met Mick Coup and saw the kind of pad training that he was doing that I realised I could get a lot more value from pad training if I put more thought into the questions of what pad drills are for and how you could get the most from using them.

Self Defense Solutions

Like any kind of self-defence training, the goal should be to make the training as realistic as possible. By that I mean that, whatever you do in training, the training should hold some kind of relevance to the type of situations you are going to be facing in the real world.

Going back to static pad drills – where the pad holder stands, usually half asleep, holding the pad aloft like a stop sign, basically passing time while he awaits his turn to strike – what relevance does that have to a real situation? When was the last time an attacker stood perfectly still in front of you and allowed you line up and fire off a shot without any resistance or attempt to avoid the strike? If that happened then the person didn't deserve to be hit in the first place.

Completely static pad training should only be used when you are first beginning to learn a particular technique. At this early stage you are not worried about application or performing the technique under pressure; your only goal is to learn the movements of the technique itself. You can't do that when the pad is moving around or other stuff is happening at the same time. So having a fixed target to strike means you can concentrate solely on body mechanics, accuracy and power generation. It also allows the pad holder or your instructor to evaluate your technique and give feedback more easily, since they are not having to worry about doing other stuff, like utilising another pad or firing off strikes themselves.

Once you get a good handle on the fundamentals of your techniques then it is time to move on to more complex drills and movements, and this is where the real creativity and innovation comes into play because you now have to think about the kinds of problems you will most likely be up against in a real situation. This brings us on to how to formulate the drills themselves.

How to Create a Pad Drill

When creating pad drills you have to start with a problem-solution mindset. Think about a typical attack scenario that might take place. What kinds of things happen in such a situation in terms of fighting? What does the other guy do? How do they attack? How do they make it difficult for you to attack them back? These are the types of questions you should ask. Look deeply at different attack scenarios. Think about your own experience or any fights that you have witnessed. Ask yourself how you can best relate your current pad training to what actually happened in those situations.

Let's take a basic highline strike—a palm strike or a right cross, it doesn't really matter. Your goal is obviously to land that strike on your attacker's head somewhere, and to do so as many times as it takes to end the situation. What might prevent you from doing that? Might your opponent throw their arms up in front of them in defence, making it more difficult for you to land a clean shot? Might your opponent move around a lot? Might he move his head so you can't hit him? I'd say that's a safe bet, wouldn't you? People don't like to be hit and they will do all they can to avoid that happening.

So we've established that the other guy is going to move around a lot and possibly flinch his head away from your strike. Wouldn't it be a good idea to practice hitting a target that doesn't want to be hit? Now we formulate a drill where the pad holder suddenly moves the pad when you go to hit it. He may pull the pad back slightly to simulate a head flinch. He may move the pad off-side to simulate an evasion. He may also move the pad towards you to simulate a distance closure. Or he may just cover one pad with the other one to simulate a covering of the head. Does that ever happen, do you think? It's a pretty safe bet that one or all of those things will happen in a real fight.

Now you are throwing shots at a pad that doesn't want to be hit, just like a real person. The level of realism and relevancy just went up considerably. Now you have to find a solution to the problem of a moving target. How can you hit a target that keeps moving? Simple really—you move with it.

If an opponent flinches their head back in reaction to your strike, you throw another one as you advance forward. Or you quickly move around to the side because your opponent has moved that way. Or you could throw an off-line strike. You are learning to track the target wherever it goes, no matter what way it moves. You are also learning to keep up offensive pressure, even if some of your strikes are far from good or even if you miss the target altogether. This is error recovery, which I talked about in my last book. You make a mistake you don't stop. You keep going. There is no resetting in a real fight. You get what you are given.

Let's look at some other examples. Would your opponent ever try to hit you back, even as you are trying to hit him? Of course he would. So how do you simulate that in a drill? Quite simply, you get the pad holder to throw shots at your head with the free pad. You will cover or block the strike and then immediately strike back again. Have the pad holder vary the timing of the shots and also the type and amount of shots thrown. You could also bring in the moving target drills to combine with this for even more realism and difficulty.

Another example. Has an attacker ever reached out and grabbed you in some way, or held you back with their free hand while trying to hit you with the other? Then have the pad holder do the same, either grabbing your shirt while you strike the pad, or shoving the free pad into your chest to keep you at a distance while you continue to strike the target pad. Again you can mix this up by having the target pad move around a lot.

How about creating space to strike, like when an opponent has completely closed you down, perhaps in an attempt to take you down or just to prevent you from striking them any further? How could you simulate this in a drill? You could start by having your partner grab a hold of you, hugging you almost. You must now find a way to create enough space so you can use your highline strike again. You could do this in a number of ways. You could simply push back off your opponent to create space that way, or you could employ elbow strikes or headbutts to force them back instead, both of which can be practiced on the pads. Either way, you will finish by highline striking the pad again.

Maybe you want to up the pressure in these drills. You could do this by bringing in two or more pad holders. Stand between the pad holders with your eyes closed. The go signal is when you are tapped or slapped by one of the pads. You will open your eyes and immediately respond to whatever the pad holder is feeding you. He may be feeding you one of the drills we mentioned earlier, perhaps moving the pad away as you try to strike. You just keep trying to hit the moving target with as many good shots as possible until you feel yourself being tapped by another pad holder. Immediately turn around to face whatever the pad holder is feeding you. This time you may be faced with the pads very close in and you will have to create space some way, just as we discussed earlier, with elbow strikes, headbutts or simply pushing them away before reverting to highline strikes.

Keep at it until you are tapped again and you have to turn around to face another pad situation. The more the pad holders mix up the problems you will be faced with the better. Not knowing what's coming next will only add to the pressure of the drill which will make it hard to think. You may even freeze sometimes as you work out what to do. This is nothing to worry about. It's normal for that to happen. You will freeze less the more you practice the drill. The whole drill should go on for a minimum of thirty seconds, but you can go on for as long as you like. Extending the drill to a minute or two minutes will add an element of stress to it as well as you struggle to keep going even though you are fatigued.

There is a myriad of ways that you can make your pad drills more relevant and more realistic. The methodology is to build the drills up in layers, adding in one component at a time. You can make the drills as complex as you like, just as long as you stick to the rule of thumb that you relate the drills to what actually happens in real situations. There is no point adding in stuff that isn't going to happen in a real situation. Always keep the end goal in mind, which is to learn to properly apply your techniques in a variety of circumstances and under various levels of pressure. The more you can do this, the more competent and prepared you will be for a real situation.

Take the time to put some thought into your pad training. There is somewhat of an art to it, especially when it comes to actually working the pads for a partner. You won't do your partner any favours by just moving the pads around in a haphazard fashion. A good pad holder will visualise the situation they are trying to create in the drill and they will use the pads to mimic as closely as possible the movements of a real person. A pad holder must therefore fully engage with the drill just as much as the striker.

We have only scratched the surface of pad drill training in this chapter. You could probably fill a book with the different combinations of drills it's possible to do. The important thing is that you understand the goals of pad drill training and the fundamental principles involved. Once you grasp these, you should be able to come up with your own forms of pad training.

Chapter 4| Improving Your Striking

The highline strike is one of the most fundamental strikes in combatives, as it is in fighting in general. It sits firmly in the high percentage bracket and as such it can be firmly relied upon to help get you out of trouble.

Think of all the fights you've ever been in. Consider all of the sport fights you've seen and those street fight videos on YouTube.

How many of those fights were finished with a highline strike?

The vast majority of them, that's how many.

It is therefore in your interests as a self defence practitioner to work hard on your highline strikes, and to make them as powerful and as effective as they can be.

When I say highline strike, I'm talking about a strike to the head, either with closed fist or open hand. Personally, I like to practice both. Despite all the discussions about closed fist techniques being bad for your hands, I still like to practice them.

Often when you are under pressure, you will default to closed fist strikes whether you want to or not. It's just one of those things. Punching seems to be a conditioned response in most people.

Whatever your preferences, the practice methods will be the same. This is what we are going to focus on in this chapter: How to practice your highline strikes so you can get maximum benefit from the practice.

Practicing With a Partner

Solo practice for striking is okay, but I believe to get the most from your practice you need a good partner to give you feedback.

Feedback is essential if you want to correctly gauge how effective your strikes really are. Partners can also spot flaws in your body mechanics that you may not even be aware of. And as we are about to see, a partner is essential for creating a *feedback loop*, but we'll get to that in a minute.

First I would like to talk briefly about the much vaunted "10,000 hour rule", which states that in order to master anything you must invest at least ten thousand hours of practice time.

While this rule seems to be true, by and large, it is only half the story. The other half of the story is that, if during those hours of practice the movements you are practicing are full of errors, you are wasting your time repeating them. You are just instilling errors into your technique and performance.

Anders Erricson, the psychologist whose research helped to spawn the aforementioned rule, has stated:

"You don't get benefits from mechanical repetition, but by adjusting your execution over and over to get closer to your goal."

"You have to tweak the system by pushing," he adds, "allowing for more errors at first as you increase your limits."

The *quality* of your practice is therefore very important when it comes to mastery and making improvements.

That's the first key to proper deliberate practice.

The second key is adding in a *feedback loop*, which, as we have said, must come in the form of a coach or partner who knows what they are doing and what to look for.

The cornerstone of effective practice is therefore engaging in that feedback loop while working with someone who has an expert eye.

Learning to Concentrate

It sounds simple. Just concentrate. Not always easy for some.

Concentration requires that you get good at controlling your attention and focus.

The only thing you should be focusing on is the task at hand, which is practicing your highline strike and focusing on whatever aspect you need to focus on. That may be getting the right recoil, or following through more, or improving your accuracy, whatever aspect of the strike needs working on.

Nothing else should be in your head at this time.

Nothing.

You should be completely in the present moment.

Daniel Goldman says:

"Paying full attention seems to boost the mind's processing speed, strengthen synaptic connections, and expand or create neural networks for what we are practicing."

So forget the rest of your life and what's going on around you (although if people are talking loudly in the background while you are trying to train you have my permission to throw a kettlebell at their heads).

Learning to concentrate is an important mental skill, and not just for practice, but also in live self-defence situations. The more switched on you are in a given situation, the quicker you will notice things and the quicker you will react to them.

Learn to focus fully on the task at hand. Your practice will improve when you do.

Establishing a Baseline for Impact

What I mean by establish a baseline is that your partner should tell you when you have hit the pad correctly, with either palm strike or closed fist.

Too much bounce on impact will result in a weak strike.

From the pad holder's point of view, there will be no penetration felt. The energy of the strike just seems to fizzle out into the pad.

Too much follow-through will also result in a weak strike because the focused impact will not be there.

From the pad holder's perspective, it will feel like the pad is being pushed or "patted" instead of struck.

For your strike to be effective, it's crucial that you get the balance right between recoil (bounce) and follow-through.

When the balance is right, the strike will feel solid. The impact should penetrate into the pad to the point where it almost hurts the hand of the pad holder.

The pad holder should be able to feel the impact on the palm of their own hand.

That's the baseline for your impact.

Your partner should tell you when the impact is there by saying *yes* or *no* after each strike.

It is up to you to get as many positive responses as possible, which will require you to concentrate.

In doing this you are practicing very deliberately, striving towards the goal of delivering correct and maximum impact each time.

It's deliberate practice with an inbuilt feedback loop.

Not Overthinking the Body Mechanics

Correct body mechanics are clearly important when it comes to striking, but sometimes I see people get so caught up in the finer points that they stiffen up through trying too hard and thinking too much about what they are doing.

Don't fall victim to overthinking.

The basic goal of a highline strike, in terms of body mechanics, is to get as much of your body weight behind the strike as possible. That's it in a nutshell.

How you do that is really up to you. Most people get how to use the hips to generate torque. It's not that hard.

Measure the effectiveness of your strike by how much impact you deliver with it, not by the body mechanics you use to deliver that impact.

If you focus more on hitting the pad correctly, as we discussed previously, the body mechanics will more or less take care of themselves.

Of course you can tweak certain movements, but only if it makes a significant difference to the effectiveness of your strike.

You are trying to hit hard. That is all.

Spending too much time on tweaking body mechanics probably isn't wise when you could be focussing more on delivering impact and learning to apply your technique in different situations. Technical lock can set in, which is where you get bogged down in tiny details to the point where you begin to lose all perspective. You lose sight of the real purpose behind doing the technique in the first place, which is just to learn to hit a target as hard as you can. If you want to spend hours on the minutiae of body mechanics, then go ahead. It's your practice time.

One further tip here is to exaggerate your movements and fully load up before you strike. This will help to counteract stress compression.

Stress compression is when your movements get shorter when you are under any kind of pressure (such as in a real fight).

If you keep your movements long in practice there will be less compression when you find yourself having to do them under pressure.

Using Your Head

It is possible to increase the power of your strikes by learning how to use your head correctly when striking.

In basic terms, you simply lead with the head by throwing it forward first (as you would when throwing an object), with everything else following behind.

Doing this seems to lead to greater impact and more bodyweight going into the strike since the head pulls the rest of the body with it, creating more momentum in the process.

You will need to try this out yourself to understand it fully.

Not Being Afraid To Fail

Just about everyone I have trained has had a tendency to be overly critical of themselves and their performance, to the point where it sometimes leads to them getting depressed and losing confidence.

This can happen if a person continually makes errors in their practice or if their strikes aren't measuring up to whatever standard they have set for themselves.

No good can come from this type of negative thinking.

You can't be afraid to fail.

You can't be afraid to repeatedly mess things up, especially in the beginning when you are just learning this stuff.

Proper deliberate practice is about working on the edge of your abilities. On that edge lies frustration and the potential to make many errors, errors that you must learn to recover from.

That edge is also where you need to be if you want to improve.

No one ever improved while remaining inside their comfort zone.

If your strike doesn't measure up for whatever reason, don't stop and go into a slump and start saying things like, *"Damn..."* like it's the end of the world.

Just do the next strike!

Forget about your previous mistake and move on immediately.

Sometimes I would ask a student to do three or four strikes in quick succession. They do the first one right and the next one would be off for whatever reason, and then they would stop and start cursing or apologising for their perceived ineptitude.

Why?

Keep going, even if you do mess up the first couple.

Just keep hitting!

You most likely will make similar mistakes in a real situation, so you'd better get used to carrying on regardless and adjusting course if necessary.

You can't reset in a real fight.

Keep your self-talk under control as well. Banish any type of negative thinking.

See your mistakes as bringing you closer to your goal.

Don't dwell or overthink.

Learn the lesson in the mistake and then move on.

Using Your Internal Energy

I'm not talking about using chi or any similar nonsense when I say use your internal energy.

I'm talking about firing up your central nervous system just before you strike and using aggression and intent in your delivery of the strike.

If you focus, you will get a visceral feel for this energy. Usually it starts in the core and travels out from there.

Learn how to conjure this energy up from inside of yourself and direct it into whatever target you are hitting.

This internal energy will help to increase the explosiveness of your strikes. I will talk more about intent and internal energy in the next chapter.

Slowing Down

Another very common mistake that I see people make when striking is that they try to do so too fast, to the point where they almost trip over themselves.

The best way to counter this is to fully focus on what you are doing and concentrate your attention on making every movement as deliberate and as effective as possible.

Your strikes will improve significantly if you can do this.

For a more detailed explanation of this, see the chapter on taking your time.

Approaching Your Training Like a Pro

If you really want results from your training then you have to take a professional approach to it.

Taking a professional approach you will put the required time and effort into your training and you will always strive to improve.

With an amateur approach you will train only when you feel like it (which won't be often) and when you do train you will hold back from giving it your all because you just can't be bothered and you think you are good enough already.

Here's Daniel Goldman again to sum up these two approaches:

"Amateurs are content at some point to let their efforts become bottom-up operations. After about fifty hours of training — whether in skiing or driving — people get to that "good-enough" performance level, where they can go through the motions more or less effortlessly. They no longer feel the need for concentrated practice, but are content to coast on what they've learned. No matter how much more they practice in this bottom-up mode, their improvement will be negligible.

"The experts, in contrast, keep paying attention top-down, intentionally counteracting the brain's urge to automatize routines. They concentrate actively on those moves they have yet to perfect, on correcting what's not working in their game, and on refining their mental models of how to play the game, or focusing on the particulars of feedback from a seasoned coach. Those at the top never stop learning: if at any point they start coasting and stop such smart practice, too much of their game becomes bottom-up and their skills plateau."

Apply these things to your practice, along with everything else in this book, and you will quickly start to see improved results.

Chapter 5| Intent

An important concept to be aware of in combatives training is the concept of intent, or *violent intent*. Intent is what fuels your actions and powers up your techniques. Without it you would be performing empty movements and there wouldn't be much point in that.

Intention itself starts with a thought and that thought leads to action. However, in the context we are discussing here, there is slightly more to intent than that.

Violent intent is having the intention to do harm to someone. In a self-defence scenario that would be your attacker. You can be certain that your attacker will have a lot of violent intent behind their actions so you need to have the same.

In fact it is this intent to do harm that often gives away a potential attacker's gameplan. One of the key tenets of awareness is being switched on enough to sense or spot that violent intent in a person before they get the chance to follow it through with violence of action. The quicker you can pick up on a person's violent intent, the more time you will have to formulate a response to it, which could mean avoiding that person, pre-empting them or, at the very least, being ready to counter their attack on you.

In a training context, intent is important because it will make your techniques much more effective if you can learn to use and channel that intent and convert it into a violent action. But how do we do this? How do we learn to stir up and channel something as intangible as intent?

Like I said, intent starts in the mind. Every time you perform a technique, a highline strike say, you should be thinking in your mind about what kind of effect you want that strike to have. This will be a split second process for most. The longer you have been training, the quicker and easier it will be for you to form your intent. In the beginning, it may take a little longer as you familiarise yourself with the process.

Every time you strike a pad you should be intending for that strike to be as effective as possible, which means hitting with full power and speed. Without a certain amount of intent behind your movements you will not reach full effectiveness with your strike. This is why intent is so important. It will help you dig deep and tap into more of your potential.

The type of thoughts that you formulate in your mind so you can stir up that intent are up to you. Do whatever works for you. The whole point of the initial thought process is to trigger your emotions. This is what thoughts do. They trigger emotions.

Have you ever found yourself dwelling on certain thoughts, only to find yourself feeling a certain way soon after? That's because your thoughts stirred up those emotions.

This is also why it is so important to keep a handle on what thoughts pass through your head, especially in self-defence scenarios. Psychological fear in these situations can trigger very debilitating emotions that will greatly hamper how you perform in such situations.

Be mindful of the thoughts you are thinking. You don't always have to engage with them. Try to let them pass by like clouds. This is isn't always possible when you are under duress, but at least if you are aware of the process at work, you stand a greater chance of getting it under control.

In this case, however, we don't want to stop our thoughts; we want to create them so we can trigger certain emotions and bodily reactions. To be honest, I'm not sure what goes on in my head before I strike. The whole process has been reduced to just a feeling and an explosion of energy. Somewhere in my mind, though, there are thoughts of doing harm and thoughts of bad intention, or else nothing would be triggered in my body. Experiment with this yourself. Find out what kinds of thoughts trigger the most intense reactions in you and stick to those thoughts.

So what kind of emotions and bodily reactions are triggered by these thoughts and intentions? Well to me it is all just energy. That's how I think of it—internal energy. For the sake of clarity, however, I'll try to pinpoint some of the emotions that make up this energy.

For sure, one of the main sources of this internal energy is aggression. This is something many people struggle with, females especially. Anytime I have trained a woman in self-defence the biggest stumbling block to progress has been their reluctance and seeming inability to tap into and use their aggression. It's just not a natural thing for most females, which is why they often struggle with it. In saying that, I have trained plenty of males who struggled just as much with the same thing. Usually though, in both cases, once we got the thought process right, the rest would fall into place.

In terms of bodily sensations, you should feel that explosion of energy somewhere in your core. Intention itself is creating something from nothing. That's what you are doing when you form an intention: you are creating something that doesn't currently exist. It is the same with aggression. The aggression itself isn't there yet. You must create it in order to bring it into being.

You can practice creating this energy just by forming intention over and over, each time feeling that energy rise up inside of you. Make like you are going to strike but don't actually perform the full movements. Hold back from striking but feel the energy that materialises inside of you, and then feel it dissipate as you relax again. This is a good way to get a feel for what is going on inside of you, and a way to practice bringing that energy – that aggression – into existence with just your will alone.

Take this a step further by practicing on the heavy bag. Do your strikes in bursts of three in rapid succession. Do so with as much violent intent as you can muster. Practicing your strikes in this way really brings out your aggression. You'll be surprised by just how much.

Neal Martin

The more you can make yourself aware of this process of energy creation, and the more you practice it, the better you will get at controlling it. That's really what it's all about, controlling that energy so you can turn it on and off at will.

I can't stress enough the importance of being able to form this kind of violent intent. If you don't have it, especially in a real situation, your strikes will not be anywhere near as effective as they should be.

In almost all self-defence scenarios, you will need a good amount of violent intent to get you through them. Without that energy to carry you through you will be overwhelmed by the energy of your opponent, which, as I mentioned, they will likely have in spades. Criminals and street thugs are experts at using bad intent to get what they want. They are experts at turning it on and off like a tap.

Think about your average mugger or street thug. They will casually approach their victims, seemingly very relaxed and not showing any signs of overt aggression. Then, at a certain point in the interview, they will suddenly explode into violence and drop their victims like a stone before the victim even knows what hit them. Then the criminal will switch off the violence again and casually flee the scene.

Violence and violent intent are tools to these people and they know how to use those tools to good effect.

You may be saying that not every situation will require you to have full violent intent. I'm not saying you should behave like a psychopath or a violent, out of control animal. I am saying, though, that you need to be able to go for it when you have too and give it all you've got.

Consider the fact that most people will not end up in very many violent confrontations and when they do it is because they have been left with no choice but to use violence to counter the threat. You aren't going to hit anyone unless you are left with no choice in the matter. If the situation is serious enough that you have to use violence to contain it, then it is serious enough for you to not hold back with whatever countermeasures you use. If you are going to do it, then do it right.

The first few altercations I ended up in when I started bouncing were an eye-opener for me. I held back somewhat when I had to hit anyone and consequently my opponents didn't go down as quickly as they should have. In fact, they came back at me even more forcefully. So an experienced bouncer I was working with at the time pulled me aside and said, *"This isn't like in the gym. If you are going to hit them don't hold back because they won't hold back on you."* His language was a lot more colourful than that but that's what he was trying to get across. He was talking about violent intent. He was telling me to hit with violent intent, which is what I'm telling you now.

So when you are in the gym and you are practicing your strikes, make sure you hit with full violent intent each and every time. I think of it as a form of nastiness. I often tell my students this: Be nasty when you hit, but also keep it controlled.

Controlled nastiness.

If you are practicing highline strikes on the pads, don't think about hitting the pad, think about trying to break your partner's hand as they hold the pad. If you are practicing a thigh kick on the pads, then it's the same thing. You are not just simply hitting the pad; you are trying to break your partner's leg. That's being nasty. Not that you will break anything, but the point is the intention is there and that intention will make your strikes more potent.

To misquote Bruce Lee: "Be nasty, my friend…"

Now let's move on to look at support skills in the next chapter.

Chapter 6|Support Skills for Better Offence and Defence

An important support skill in combatives is the ability to use the hands and arms in a tactical manner that involves more than just striking.

Your arms are your first line of defence when you get attacked, and as such they can be used in different ways before any strike is thrown. You can also continue to use your hands in various ways to set up your strikes.

Even before an attack happens, the arms are used to control space between you and whatever threat you are facing, as in the fence concept.

What I want to talk about here is the continuation of that fence concept even after an attack has begun. It is one of the things that I always try to emphasise with students, the need to always keep the arms out in front in a fluid guard position. From that position, a number of different applications will flow, which we will look at now.

The Initial Guard Position

There really isn't much more to say on this that hasn't already been said a thousand times before, though the importance of this guard position cannot be over-emphasised. It's your first line of defence between you and your attacker. Without that defence in place, a difficult situation can get even harder if your personal space is invaded and the other guy is on top of you, so to speak.

This position is also important because it will help you to underscore your assertiveness. As I've discussed in my previous books, it is important to control the pre-fight phase by drawing a metaphorical line in the sand for your opponent. You must communicate to your aggressor with your body language and choice of words that if they step over that line they will not do so without consequences.

Drilling this initial guard position is easy enough. Just have a partner try to invade your space and use your hands to push back off them while stepping back or around. No need to try to hold your ground unless you can't move back for some reason.

Also, the higher your hands, the harder it will be for the other person to hit you, and the quicker you will be able to pre-empt should you need to.

Defensive Movements

If your opponent should attack first in any way you need to be able to use your hands/arms to defend against the attack. I'm not talking about blocking here, at least not in the traditional sense. To all intents and purposes though, this is what you are doing, blocking the incoming attack and preventing it from hitting you (too much).

The most effective ways to do this seem to be based upon an initial flinch reaction. Again, much has been said about the so-called startle-flinch reaction but it is nothing more than your mind saying, "HOLY SHIT!" and your body following suit by flinching away from whatever attack has come.

There are quite a few different variations on this flinch reaction and which one you use will be up to you. I'm sure it's possible to make them all work with practice.

I'm not fond of anything that involves covering by clamping the arms around the head (although sometimes this may be necessary, especially in the case of multiple opponents). I'm not saying this isn't a useful tactic, but I prefer to keep my arms out in front of me whenever possible, allowing the lead arm to absorb most of the attack. I'll flinch away and throw my lead arm up and out, so in the case of a punch, it will mostly hit my arm. If more punches come I keep both arms moving out in front so I can deflect, block, parry or trap my opponent's punching arm.

The main reason I do this is so I can quickly strike when I get the chance. This isn't so easy when your arms are clamped to your head.

What I have discovered about defending against attacks like punches is that there are no real fixed techniques to use. Under pressure, it is a case of flinching and blocking/covering. This process tends to pan out differently each time, depending on the type of attack and how good or bad your reaction has been. Sometimes you fail and get hit. Put the full contact gear on and you will soon discover this.

What is more important than how you initially deal with an incoming attack is how quickly you go on the offensive afterwards.

Regardless of what shape your startle-flinch reaction took, you must be swift in moving forward with your own attack, otherwise you are going to end up on the back foot, losing ground until you are overwhelmed.

In terms of drilling this, you can start by having a partner simply try to hit you with a pad so you can practice whatever defence you are working on, be it blocking with the lead arm out or by clamping it to the side of your head before you strike back. I suggest you also practice defence with safety helmets on so you can both go hard. Your partner should attack hard and you should try to get on the offensive as quickly as possible before they get the chance to throw any more strikes.

I find working full contact in this way helps develop your fighting instincts much more. We will discuss this aspect of fighting drills in a later chapter.

Indexing, Checking, Grabbing and Controlling

As I've said, it's important to keep the hands out in front throughout the duration of the fight whenever possible.

If an opponent is moving in towards you (as they will be as they are trying to hit you) you also need to be able to utilise your lead arm to check, grab, control and index.

Indexing as a concept you should already be familiar with, especially if you have read my other books. To recap, indexing is using the lead arm to give you a reference point so you can strike with accuracy. If you can touch your opponent you can also hit him. Indexing will also help your body mechanics, helping to form a solid and stable structure from which to strike.

This is why I like to keep my arms out in front and moving fluidly, because you are always feeling out the space and always indexing to back up your strikes.

Beyond indexing we have checking, which I always find very useful. You don't want any attacker in on top of you, so checking them as they come in is a very effective way to keep them at bay or to redirect them off-side.

Often an attacker will use their own lead arm in a similar way, keeping it out front as they strike. In that case, you can slap their arm down or away from you, which will make it easier for your strikes to get through.

Grabbing and controlling are two other aspects that can prove useful, depending on the circumstances. I tend to utilise these more when I am in close and I want to get a grip on my opponent.

It's hard to say exactly when you will use these applications in a fight. In the main they are used spontaneously.

A good drill though is to have a partner attack you with boxing gloves on or else wear the protective gear. Have them come forward and attack while you practice using your arms to check, grab, control, index and strike or whatever the circumstances require. Practice creating gaps, clearing paths and getting some sort of index to strike. This kind of practice will hone your fighting instincts so that these support techniques come naturally to you after a while. Again I'll discuss this further in a later chapter.

Alternatively, isolate the different components and come up with different pad drills to practice them. Follow up the pad drills with the full contact drills so you can practice applying them under pressure.

Neal Martin

Chapter 7|Three Major Flaws in Combatives Training and How to Fix Them

When it comes to combatives training, not all roads lead to Rome. In fact, some of the roads people tread lead to nowhere at all in terms of getting good results. To get good results, combatives training has to be structured in a certain way. The problem is that many people who profess to train in combatives don't know what that way is.

Much of what passes for combatives and self-defence training is marred by ignorance and indulgence. Many people are just unable to resist the gratification that comes from indulging their whims and desires. Consequently, an awful lot of combatives "systems" out there are just a total mess, ungoverned by either rhyme or reason.

For some reason, in this industry people think it is okay to do what they want and teach what they want without even considering if what they are doing is correct. And by correct I mean does what they are doing lead to tangible results? Can they prove that their training is effective? In a lot of cases, the answer is no.

If you took the people who train in these faulty and indulgent systems and you put them in a professional environment where they had to use their "skills" (such as law enforcement, security, military roles, even street fighting) they would most likely fail miserably in trying to implement their training into these environments. This is because the training methods and objectives are way off in most cases, which leads to the wrong outcomes.

It would take another book to detail all the ways in which combatives and self-defence in general are incorrectly taught and trained, so in this chapter I'm going to highlight just three major flaws that I see in a lot of combatives training out there. These flaws are big enough that they effectively mess up everything else, rendering most training useless. So let's look at these flaws now.

Too much emphasis on role-play and padded suit drills.

This is one of the biggest flaws that currently exist in combatives training. Think about combatives and the image that will most likely pop into your head is of a guy wearing a padded suit with a huge helmet on his head as he "attacks" some trainee.

On the surface, scenario training with padded suits seems like a great idea, but in reality this is rarely the case. Think about the way in which most of these drills are done: The padded man ambles up to the trainee mouthing some nonsense like, *"What the fuck are you looking at? You want some, do you?"* before launching into the worst attack you've ever seen. The trainee, meanwhile, launches their own (often sloppy and uncoordinated) counter attack and the padded assailant makes a show of being overwhelmed by the ferocity of the trainee's attack, helpfully backtracking as the trainee bangs that huge helmet with a few largely ineffectual palm strikes or pulled punches. Afterwards everybody claps and pats themselves on the back like they are at a Tony Robbins seminar. *"What a rush! That was so real!"*

No! There was nothing real about that scenario! It was all pre-planned and it looked like a fight scene from a really bad action movie. Nothing about it was realistic. Yet everyone involved thought it to be the height of realism. There may have been some kind of buzz involved, some minor adrenaline rush, but that doesn't make the drill any less unrealistic. It was a feel-good drill, an ego massage, that's it. Would such a drill make you a better operator, a better fighter? Not likely.

Unfortunately, this is how quite a lot of people in combatives train. They take a few techniques, drill those techniques for a short while (usually wrongly) and then "pressure test" them against the padded suit guy before going home, certain that they are now fully prepared and ready for action if they ever find themselves in trouble.

It takes more than a few ill-conceived and sloppy pressure tests to make someone operational. And by the way, I use the terms "operator" and "operational" not in a tactical tourist sense (please) but in a purely practical and functional sense. I don't like the term "fighting" as it has too many negative connotations and it also implies duelling, which is not what combatives is about. Combatives is about learning to operate and use your skills in different situations, hence the term "operator". It's a much more apt term for what we are trying to achieve through training. Just don't go all Jason Bourne when you hear the term, for God's sake. Anyway, moving on...

In the same bracket we have the whole scenario training thing where you have to method act your way through some made up situation. Instructors will say things like, *"Okay, you're tired, you're just home from work, you haven't been feeling well all day and you get home to find six guys there waiting for you..."* or *"You're in the cinema and an old lady jumps you from behind because she's pissed at the sound of your popcorn munching... What are you gonna do?"*

Okay, maybe not quite as ludicrous as that last one, but not far off it! Between the padded suit drills and these silly scenarios, people have wandered off into fantasy land again, haven't they?

These drills can certainly *feel* very realistic in the training hall, but in the training hall you can bend reality whatever way you like it. People do it all the time. So the fact that these drills feel real in the gym does not under any circumstances mean they are viable training methods. In most cases they are simply a feel-good buzz for the participants.

This is not to say that full contact drills cannot be useful. Force on force training can be useful of course (as we will see later), and indeed it is necessary at some point. Trainees need to feel what it is like to go up against a fully resisting opponent. They also need to experience the feeling of shock and awe that comes from being thrust into a sudden-violence situation. Most padded suit drills fail to meet these two criteria. The attacker doesn't usually offer much resistance and there is too much build up for any shock and awe to occur.

For shock and awe you need to look towards Mick Coup's Live Drill, where two participants clash head on and GLF (Go Like Fuck!), as Mick would say, for just a few seconds before being pulled apart again. There is no dialogue exchange or squaring off, just sudden violence that ends just as suddenly (like most real world scenarios).

With other force on force drills you can have two (or more) participants start in various different positions and go from there, for instance, one person on the ground, the other standing, or both in a standing grappling position. Both participants would obviously be going as hard as their equipment will allow; pretty much full contact. Throughout, an instructor would provide coaching, very much like the way an MMA fighter is coached from the side-lines.

That's two examples of how to make good use of your padded suits and also your training time. Both these methods are far more preferable and far more useful than the whole *what are you looking at?* one-sided affairs that pass for pressure testing and scenario training.

To be honest, your training time would be much better spent training the fundamentals, doing simple pad drills that are based on occurrences in actual fights and leaving the full contact stuff until the fundamental fighting skills are firmly enough grasped. But more on that shortly. Let's look at the next major flaw first.

Not enough repeat and/or deliberate practice.

It's quite simple really: The sharper your tools are the more effective they are going to be. Dull tools don't do a very good job.

To have effective tools (effective techniques) you need to sharpen those tools on a continuous basis, which means doing countless reps of each technique. Most martial arts and self-defence practitioners already know this, but still very few actually do it.

There could be many reasons as to why the fundamental techniques are not practiced enough. It really doesn't matter. You only need to know one thing: *If you want results from your training you have to go beyond the norm when it comes to how you practice.*

You have to practice as *deliberately* as possible. It's not just a matter of banging out a few hundred reps of a technique. It's a simple matter to do that. What is harder, and what is far more effective, is to try to make each rep as perfect as you can make it. This means that each rep must be focused, powerful and correctly formed, as efficient and as effective as you can make it. What's more, you should be aiming to do each rep with as little conscious thought involved as possible. There is no room for overthinking. Each movement should be instinctual almost, not laboured and over-thought. The goal is to get better all the time and to instil the technique as deeply as possible.

Many people avoid this kind of practice because they don't see it as being sexy enough. They want the cool stuff, not the boring stuff. Well, you know what? It's the boring stuff that makes you good. The cool sexy stuff just makes you useless, that's all there is to it.

If you understand the nature of what you are trying to achieve in your training then you shouldn't run away from simple, repetitive practice. If you avoid this kind of training then you obviously don't want to *be* good, you just want to *look* good; you want to feed your ego and your fantasies—or you're just too damn stupid to recognise bullshit when you see it. As you're reading this, I'll assume you don't fall into the latter category.

Remember also that repetitive practice of single techniques is just a part of the overall process of training. Once you have fully grasped the fundamentals of a technique then you must work on being able to use it in context. But even with this type of contextual practice, the rules of repetition still apply. You can never practice these things too much, even drills, either live or with pads.

The goal of repeat practice of the fundamentals is not to turn you into a mindless robot, but into someone who knows how to use their tools effectively in varying circumstances. Keep the bigger picture in mind as you train and know why you are doing what you are doing.

This is purposeful practice. To quote Matthew Syed from his book, *Bounce*:

"The practice sessions of aspiring champions have a specific and never-changing purpose: progress. Every second of every minute of every hour, the goal is to extend one's mind and body, to push oneself beyond the outer limits of one's capacities, to engage so deeply in the task that one leaves the training session, literally, a changed person."

Self Defense Solutions

This kind of purposeful practice begins with repeat practice of the fundamentals. It does not entail practicing some move a few times before moving on to the next one. Purposeful practice is how professional athletes train. It is how you should train as well.

Not using systemised training methods.

If you have ever tried to write a novel then you will know how important having an outline is, a basic structure to follow. Try to write a novel without an outline and I guarantee you will fail miserably. Your novel, if it even gets finished, will be all over the place. It won't make much sense. It will be full of holes. A good read is one thing it won't be.

When it comes to self-defence and combatives training, most people approach it like someone trying to write a novel with no outline or pre-thought out structure. In short, the training is all over the place. As a result, most people who train this way are also all over the place.

If you wanted to build a machine would you hastily cobble together a load of random parts and hope the machine worked in the end? Of course not, you'd draw up a blueprint first, decide exactly what parts you will need and then go about assembling those parts in the correct order and in the correct way. Following this approach you will end up with a fully working, efficient and effective machine, capable of doing the job it was built to do.

This is the same approach you need to take to your training as well. You need a system that is going to build a good operator. The system must make logical sense and it must be based on truth. It also must produce tangible results, results that can be measured to a large degree.

I'm not going to get into details here on what should be in this system (read my *Combatives Instruction* book for basic guidance in this area). Suffice to say, a system is not a collection of someone's favourite techniques. That's going back to the random machine building again. A true system requires a bit more thought than that.

And actually there it is, the fix for any training flaw you can think of: *Put a bit more thought into it!*

Now staying on a similar vein, let's look at bad training habits.

Chapter 8|Bad Training Habits

Quite often in training we can develop bad habits that negatively impact our performance in some way, not to mention slow down our progress. Such habits can also bleed out into real life.

A habit that I had for many years was unthinkingly closing to grappling distance when someone attacked me. This came from years of Jujitsu training, which, in general, is all about closing down an opponent. This tactic seemed like a good idea in training, because you are not only closing down the attack but also getting control of your opponent.

When I started working doors, however, it quickly became clear that this tactic wasn't always the most effective response. I may have closed down the attack but things often got very messy after that and a lot of the time I ended up on the floor with people, struggling to get back to my feet again. If I hadn't been so quick to close distance in the first place I wouldn't have ended up on the floor.

So pretty quickly I realised I had to change tactics. Not only is it bloody exhausting wrestling with someone, it's also risky. A few times I was very lucky not to get badly hurt (from third parties) when I hit the deck with some guy. Eventually I learned to keep my distance and strike if I had to, rather than go rushing in. It wasn't easy breaking that habit. My entire approach to training had to change in order for me to do that. (Being completely honest, it is still a habit that is there, but I am more aware of it now and better able to control it.)

That's an extreme example of a bad training habit. Most unwanted training habits are small things, but small things that can have a big impact on the way that you perform. If you want to be at the top of your game then these negative habits need fixing.

So in this chapter I'm going to outline a three step process for finding and fixing any negative training habits you might have. It's actually a very simple process, but one that will require a bit of work on your part.

Step 1: Identifying the Problem

Obviously we have to start by identifying the problem. You may be aware of your bad training habits by now, or you may not. A lot of the time we are indeed aware of many of our bad habits but they are so low down on our awareness spectrum as to be hardly there at all, at least in our own minds.

We tend to wilfully ignore our bad habits. The only time we take note of them is when they play a part in messing up a drill or when they emerge at the wrong time in a fight. Then we vow to iron the problem out, but we rarely do. And so the cycle repeats itself.

If you know about your bad habits but aren't doing anything about them then you need to look at why this is. Do you think they will clear up over time or even go away by themselves, as if by magic? Or are you just not bothered by them that much?

In the latter case, I'd be bothered by them if I knew they were affecting my performance in some way. Like I said in the previous chapter, the point of training is to progress and get better, so why wouldn't you want to fix the problems that are likely hampering that progress? If you are serious about your training then you should resolve to fix those problems and habits that are having a negative impact on your performance and progress.

In the former case ... come on. These things aren't going to clear themselves up are they? They aren't going to magically disappear at some point. They will remain with you always until you do something about them.

It is, of course, slightly daunting when you first consider trying to work out and change a bad habit; all that work and frustration, the hours of conscious and deliberate practice. It can be a little off-putting. But it has to be done. If you are staying true to your intentions of wanting to get better then you will face the discomfort and get to work.

If you have already identified your bad habits, you can move on to the next step. If you haven't fully identified what needs correcting then you need to look at your training, examine it until you find something that needs fixing, something that is hampering your performance and something that, if fixed, will have a positive impact on your training.

You usually won't have to think too hard. Most of us have plenty of bad training habits, probably more than we would care to admit. Find one that's going to have the biggest impact on your training if corrected. That's the one you are going to work on. If you are having trouble finding your most pressing bad habit, just ask your instructor. They no doubt will have a long list!

One example of something that I worked on is left/right transitions while striking. Like a lot of people, I was in the habit of striking predominately with my right hand. Consequently the left hand often got neglected in practice. So if I was doing pad drills and I was striking off the right, when the opposite pad was suddenly presented, quite often I would just jab with the left hand instead of changing my feet so I could strike off the back hand. That was the habit I needed to change, jabbing with the left instead of utilising footwork to strike off the back hand. Nothing really wrong with lead arm strikes per se, but you get more power off the back hand. So that option should take preference whenever possible. Plus, such drills are also about taking you out of your comfort zone (striking comfortably of the strong side all the time), so practice of this type does you good.

Step 2: Deciding How to Fix the Problem

Whatever your bad habit, problem or weakness is you must decide how you are going to fix it. This begins by first being conscious of the problem. You must be aware of it while you are training and try to correct it or prevent it at all times. Sometimes this isn't enough, however, especially if the habit is deeply ingrained and has become automatic. In that case, you will need to drill down a little deeper to isolate the problem itself.

An easy way to do this is to simply come up with a drill or form of practice that allows you to only work on the specific problem. A weakness for many people is working off the left side as I said, so the solution to that would be to simply force yourself to practice a lot more off the left side. Of course this will feel awkward and frustrating, but if you keep practising you will get better. If you can do a few hundred reps of a technique in one session, counting only the reps that are spot on and discarding the rest, then you will quickly see a significant improvement in your technique. Your goal then would be to schedule regular practice sessions like this until you get comfortable and competent working off the left.

The process isn't much different for any other bad habit or problem you might have. Simply isolate it and consciously work on changing it. Eventually you will have to think about your movements less and less and the new way of doing things will become the norm. It's just mindful practice.

Another example I can give you would be using your index hand to grab the pad or the wrist of the pad holder while striking. This often happens when people try to index the target but end up grabbing it instead. I do it myself sometimes. It is not a good habit to have since you will not be able to grab an attacker in the same way, so it doesn't make sense to grab the pads like that. It's unrealistic.

So how do you fix such a habit? Again, just be conscious of it first of all, and then come up with little drills that isolate the problem. In this case you might simply practice indexing a pad or some other target, over and over, making sure only your fingers stick to the target and that you don't grab it. After that you might drill slowly, indexing and striking a target. All this will slowly ingrain in you the new habit of sticky fingers rather than grabbing. Finally you will move on to full-on pad drills to test if the new way of doing things has stuck. You will still try to be conscious of what you are doing to an extent. If you catch yourself grabbing the target just resolve not to do it again and continue trying to use just sticky fingers to index. Eventually the new habit will be ingrained and you won't have to think about it at all.

You may not have that problem. Your problem or habit may be different, but the process of fixing it is still the same. You will still need a plan to fix it.

Step 3: Fixing the Problem

This is the simplest step and also the hardest because it requires a good deal of work and effort. Once you have worked out how you are going to fix your problem you must then go about fixing it. This means doing the drills, putting the practice time in, maintaining mindfulness during practice and sticking at it until the bad habit, weakness or problem is ironed out.

As well as being mindful of your own practice you should also enlist the help of a training partner or instructor to provide you with feedback (remember how important to progress this is?). Sometimes they will see things that you miss or let you know when you have fallen unconsciously back into the bad habit again.

Trusting the Process

Bad training habits can be changed but you have to be honest about them first and acknowledge that you have them. Then you have to come up with the right plan to change them and stick to executing that plan. Trust the process and you will eventually iron out whatever problems you may have.

It comes down to deliberate practice again. Purposeful practice can be frustrating but ultimately it is this kind of practice that will improve your training and get you better results.

So say it: Purposeful, deliberate practice will get me better results.

Keep repeating that until it is burned into your brain.

And don't forget to actually practice—often.

Chapter 9| Live Fight Training and Developing Fighting Instincts

One of the major problems in self-defence training has always been the problem of how to go from pad drill training to live fight training whilst still trying to retain some semblance of reality. The major problem with this is how to conduct the fight training without letting it descend into ordinary dojo sparring, where two opponents face off and then begin to dance around each other and feel each other out, every now and then moving in to attack. The attack parts of these drills are fine. It's the dancing around in between that is the problem. In a real street fight, very rarely do two people dance around in that manner. It's usually just a clash of fists with each opponent trying to put the other down as quickly as possible.

In self defence training, there needs to be some kind of live fighting, that much is certain. If the only experience of fighting that a trainee has had is striking pads then they are going to be at a severe disadvantage if they have to face someone outside the gym who has fought in the street many times.

There are things about fighting that you can only learn through fighting, such as what it feels like to have someone try to hit you or wrestle you to the ground, or how hard it is to hit a moving opponent. Those are things that can only be experienced by going up against a fully resisting opponent.

So the question is: How can we conduct live fight drills that don't contain all the pointless dancing around and feeling out that exists in traditional dojo sparring? And also how can we insure they are not one-sided affairs?

Some instructors have done a good job in answering these questions and have come up with innovative ways to meet the above criteria. You have Mick Coup's live drills, which I talked about in my last book and also Southnarc who conducts similar force on force drills in his Shivworks system.

I have worked on this problem myself and I have come up with a couple of different ways to conduct live fighting that I have found to be quite beneficial when it comes to getting students used to the pressure of a real fight.

The drills that I use are primarily designed to work on developing a person's fighting instincts, something that I touched upon in an earlier chapter. The shock and awe aspect is therefore a secondary concern in these drills. My main concern in formulating the drills was to allow participants to work on their spontaneity while under pressure.

There are a few ways in which you can start these drills. Experiment and see what works best for you. Some suggestions might be for you and your partner to face each other with eyes closed – upon the go signal, you will both immediately attack one another – or you could begin by standing back to back. The point of starting like this is to prevent any kind of squaring off which is what would happen if you started the drill like a normal sparring bout.

Once the drill begins, the point is to keep attacking your opponent (both of you), trying to land as many shots as possible before the allotted time is up or before you get pulled apart. I suggest keeping the bouts to just a few seconds to create a sense of urgency. If it goes on too long there will be a tendency for both of you to start dancing around and feeling each other out. That's not really what we want from these drills. We want to create the pressure of having to end things quickly, just like in a real fight.

In saying that, you can also extend the length of the drills. In that case you wouldn't be worrying too much about ending things quickly. This would be more of an opportunity to practice your fighting skills, such as controlling your opponent, capitalising on openings and mistakes made by your opponent by putting in strikes wherever possible and also maybe applying takedowns and chokes if the opportunity presents itself. If the fight goes to the ground then you both continue until time is called or one gets the better of the other and finishes the fight in some way, even if that means getting up and escaping.

I find these extended bouts to be an ideal opportunity to practice your close-in skills. Normally, after a few seconds there is a clash and you will both end up in grappling range. Not that you have to grapple, mind you. You can also strike from that range or try to create distance again so you can land better strikes.

Another scenario you can begin with is for both of you to start on the ground, perhaps with one of you holding down the other. Upon the go signal, you will both begin to fight from that position, trying to land strikes and create an opportunity to get back to your feet again. This drill isn't really about grappling as such, although you can practice getting to a position from which to strike or control your opponent while you get back up again.

Like I said, these drills are basically very short sparring drills without the dancing around. They are an opportunity for both partners to practice using their skills in a pressurised environment, and also practice fighting in a brawling context if things did get that far in a real situation, which it often does. Ideally you should finish a real fight in just seconds, but for various reasons that doesn't always happen. If a clash happens and brawling begins it is good to know how to handle that kind of situation.

The other main goal of these drills is so you can practice your techniques in a spontaneous manner, which you will have to do in a real situation anyway. Trying to land strikes against someone who is also doing the same and who is moving around a lot isn't easy. You can only practice this aspect of fighting so much with pad drills. With the fighting drills we are discussing here, you will find the whole experience of trying to land good shots a lot more difficult and frustrating. This is why it is good to do these kinds of drills on a regular basis.

These drills can also show up holes in your game. If you continually find yourself freezing when in close then you know you need to work more on fighting from that position. Maybe you need to work on elbow strikes more to drive your opponent back, or maybe you need to work on controlling your opponent better at that range. Whatever is lacking, your instructor will see it and tell you if you don't know yourself.

Remember that these drills represent just one aspect of training. They are not the be all and end all of combatives training. Be sure to balance such drills out by doing plenty of pad work and dedicated technique work. If you don't take the time to learn the fundamentals of fighting and good technique, these live drills won't do you much good. You'll be a mess under pressure. Use the drills at the right time, when the fundamentals have been firmly enough grasped.

Neal Martin

Chapter 10|Reality Dyslexia

I read an article once in which the author was talking about punching someone on the nose. He gave a very detailed and eloquent description of this: the instant pain, the explosion of blood from the nostrils, the watering of the eyes, the force of the blow causing the recipient to stagger back, both hands clamped over their injured appendage, groaning as blood seeped through their fingers, the fight gone out of them.

This same author then went on to state that such a reaction is pretty much par for the course when someone gets whacked on the nose, like the above reaction is guaranteed.

Regardless of whether the author of said article was overstating his case or not (and I think he probably was), his assertion that a blow to the nose will *always* have the same effect only draws attention to a more widespread and insidious malaise that permeates the vast majority of the reality self-defence scene.

I'm talking about reality dyslexia. Not my term, regrettably, someone else's. Regardless of origin, the term is still very apt and perfectly describes the thinking and outlook of many people, especially those involved in 'reality' self-defence.

The aforementioned article is a good starting point from which to discuss this condition. Why?

Because only reality dyslexia would cause someone to say that if you hit a guy in the nose they will always react in the same way, therefore you can always rely on this to happen.

That's a bit like saying that it's okay to swim in shark infested waters because if you punch a shark in the nose it will always swim away and leave you alone. Care to guarantee that one?

Dyslexic Reality versus Real Reality

The fact is, you can't assume anything when it comes to fighting and self-defence, most of all how your opponent is going to react when you hit them.

Neal Martin

An assumption like that creates a dual reality: *Dyslexic Reality* and *Real Reality*.

In the dyslexic version there is how you would like or how you suppose a person would react to certain techniques. In this version, every punch would have a devastating effect on your opponent; every hit would be a perfect knockout. Every strike to the eyes would be eye-wateringly incapacitating; every kick to the groin would have your opponent flying back onto their knees in agonising pain. Similarly, things like throws and joint locks would work just the way they do in the gym.

In the other version of reality, the one that most people in the world inhabit, things would go quite differently. Not every strike would have a devastating effect and every punch thrown would not guarantee a knockout. Eye strikes would not result in your opponent staggering back with their hands over their eyes and screaming, "MY EYES! MY EYES!" Throws and joint locks would hardly get a look in.

When you put it in those terms, it can seem quite unlikely that anyone would think like that, but many people do. Reality dyslexia has a way of creeping in almost unnoticed.

Before you know it, you start to believe that your techniques are going to have the same effect every single time. They might do, but the chances of that being the case are slim to none.

The fact is that people in fights absorb so-called devastating blows all the time like they are nothing.

Pre-emptive strikes don't always result in immediate knockouts and attacks to 'vital points' like eyes, throat and groin often have no discernible effect against a fully adrenalized and determined opponent (we will discuss vital points in the next chapter).

So how do you counter this faulty thinking? What's the cure for reality dyslexia?

Beliefs and Assumptions

Firstly you must look at the beliefs and assumptions you hold regarding your training. When you find out what they are, ask yourself the following question:

Are my beliefs and assumptions about my training based on solid fact, and have those facts been proven?

If one of your beliefs is that your techniques will work perfectly under all circumstances, what proof exists to back this up?

Have you tested all of your techniques under all circumstances?

Can you even assert with proof that when you punch someone in the nose they will react in the same way every time?

The answer to both those questions is obviously going to be no. So on what basis do some people hold these beliefs to be true?

Think of the techniques that are taught in most self-defence classes. How many of those techniques would stand up to the kind of scrutiny we are talking about here?

What proof exists that these techniques do as advertised? What proof exists that these techniques work even some of the time?

Usually none in both cases.

Yet people teach them and train them like they are rock solid truths, without a shred of evidence that this is the case.

When you consider that there is potentially a lot at stake in the situations these techniques are supposed to be used in, I don't think I'm being unfair in asking for a little proof that they do what they say on the tin.

I'd say the efficacy of a technique is a pretty big prerequisite when it comes to self-defence training.

The stuff has to stand a chance of working for most people, otherwise what is the point?

But back to dangerous assumptions…

What happens when you have been training for a one punch knockout and then one day you use it and the other guy doesn't go down?

If you haven't trained to immediately follow up on that punch then you are going to freeze and a very pissed off opponent is going to hit you back really hard, ironically maybe knocking you out in the process.

Generally speaking, you should of course have a certain amount of faith in your abilities and in the techniques that you use. If you don't have that level of confidence in yourself and your abilities then you will struggle against an adversary who does have that confidence and faith in their abilities.

Remember that most predators and thugs have had a lot of practice doing what they do and using the techniques and tactics that help them take down their victims as quickly and as brutally as possible. For that reason, you had better make sure that your shit's really together.

But that doesn't mean that you should make dangerous assumptions about yourself, your skills or your abilities.

Sticking to the high percentage techniques is a good start when it comes to avoiding reality dyslexia.

Train the stuff that has actually been proven to work and resist the temptation to go down the path of whimsy or indulgence.

Unlike scientists, who actively set out to disprove their own theories, many people in the reality self-defence game do the opposite, and set out to *prove* their own shaky theories and assumptions.

People can convince themselves of anything given enough time.

If a large portion of the world population can convince themselves there is a god who created the universe and who looks out for all of its inhabitants, and do so without any concrete proof whatsoever, then it's no surprise that many self-defence practitioners can convince themselves of the efficacy of certain techniques without any proof whatsoever.

Reality dyslexia pervades the martial arts/self-defence worlds like a sickness.

When you objectively examine what actually works a high percentage of the time in a self-defence situation then you have no choice but to acknowledge that the majority of what is taught as self-defence simply isn't self-defence, and is instead self-indulgent and ignorance/ego based nonsense.

When I look at a self-defence technique I don't care where it originated from or which celebrity instructor 'invented' or teaches it.

The measure of a technique is not based on where it came from or who teaches it, but on what it can do. End of story.

The minute you allow concessions based on favouritism of some kind, assumptions begin to creep in and suddenly you have a bout of full blown reality dyslexia on your hands.

After all, if you have no concrete proof that something works (beyond working on compliant partners in training or less than worthy opponents in a real situation) then you are forced to make assumptions instead.

Assumption replaces proof.

How different would the world of science be if that where the abiding philosophy? Every crack pot theory in the world would be held up as fact.

But that doesn't happen in the scientific community. Instead, scientists posit the most likely theory, which is based on much testing and examination, before going on to try to find an even more likely theory.

Nothing is set in stone in science. If the facts change, so do the theories.

In the self-defence world, even if the facts change, the theories stay the same.

Objective reality doesn't come into it.

Self-defence should only be based on what is known to work a high percentage of the time. Assumptions shouldn't come into it.

As the saying goes: Assumption is the mother of all fuck-ups.

Those are words that should be written on the wall of every self-defence gym in the world.

Now staying along the same lines, let's examine the beliefs surrounding the so-called vital attack points.

Chapter 11|Vital Attack Points

Vital attack points are those areas on the human body that are deemed to be most vulnerable to attack. They are weak spots on the body – that's how they are put across anyway – areas such as eyes, throat, ears, nose, groin etc., etc. The thinking surrounding vital attack points is that, no matter what size your attacker is, they will still be vulnerable to attack in these areas.

I'm not doubting that these areas on the human body are indeed vulnerable, but does that automatically make them the best areas to attack?

Not necessarily, in my opinion.

Let's take the eyes. You will often hear advice like, "Go for the eyes! If he can't see, he can't fight!" or "He may be twenty stone of muscle, but he doesn't have twenty stone of muscle in his eyes! "

Fair enough. Let's take the first point of you can't see, you can't fight. If you have ever done blindfolded drills, you will know that it is perfectly possible to fight without sight. As long as you have some kind of index like a hand on the other person, you can fight almost as well as when you can actually see.

As a quick test, close your eyes and index a pad, then hit the pad. You will hit it every time. This is because you don't need to see what you are doing; you only need to *feel* what you are doing.

Taking away an opponent's sight is a good tactic, but only as a temporary measure so you can distract them long enough to line them up for a strike to the head.

As for the second point, the eyes are indeed quite soft and vulnerable. But they are also surprisingly resilient and can take a remarkable amount of punishment before they start to get really damaged. I've never gouged an eye out of its socket, but I'd wager it isn't as easy as some people think. I'd also wager that most people who talk about gouging out eyeballs from their sockets wouldn't have the internal capacity to do so.

For attacking the eyes, the common attack is to use the thumbs to press into the eye sockets. From a standing position, most people will struggle their way out of this eventually, which is why eye gouging is better used as more of a transition technique rather than a finishing move.

It's an excellent technique when someone is right in on you and you need to create space in order to strike, but that's about as far as it goes. Of course it is possible to inflict real damage to the eyes if you know what you're doing, but for common fight situations, it's unlikely that you will need to inflict permanent eye damage on your attacker, unless you don't mind getting done for GBH.

The throat is another surprisingly resilient 'weak spot'. The old web hand strike is often cited as being the best way to strike the throat. Again though, such a strike is unlikely to stop a determined opponent. Indeed, enough people have tested this technique by now that we know it isn't nearly as devastating as some believe. As such it is only useful as a set up strike.

But in saying that, why do it at all? Why not just go straight for the head? A full force punch to the throat may be a different matter and could potentially be very damaging, perhaps even lethal. But why use such a strike, unless the other guy had a knife or similar lethal weapon? It could land you in jail.

How about clawing techniques that attack the eyes and throat? Unpleasant, I'm sure, but hardly enough to stop a determined attacker. Only useful as distractions or for creating space so you can transition into more forceful techniques.

Moving on to the groin. Is a kick to the groin a fight finisher? You would think so, but it usually isn't. We've all heard enough times about people absorbing such blows easily. How many times have you caught a kick to the groin in sparring and still managed to fight on? I've lost count of how many times this has happened to me. Now factor in adrenaline and the will to survive in a real situation and you can easily see how groin shots can be ineffective. I'm not saying you shouldn't use them; they can still prove useful if preceded or followed by other strikes elsewhere.

There are many more so called vital attack points as displayed on one of those posters that used to hang on the wall of every dojo back in the day, but the fact is you'd be wasting your time with most of them. Trying to target specific and small areas on a person's body in the franticness of a fight is difficult enough. It is even more difficult to do so with any real effect. Perhaps you could do so if you were supremely skilled and highly experienced, but the average person isn't any of those things.

Targeting these areas on a compliant partner in the gym can make attacking such areas seem effective. But when you factor in adrenaline, sheer aggression, possibly alcohol and drugs, plus the fact that the other guy doesn't give a shit about what you are doing to him and will absorb any and all pain that you inflict on him, these vital attack points don't seem as deadly or as effective anymore. They are merely distractions at best, and at worst a way to further antagonise the other guy.

So what's the alternative? Ironically it is to attack another vital point on the body, and the biggest one at that—the head!

It has been proven over and over again that hitting your attacker in the head is the most efficient way to finish a fight. Everyone knows this from their own experience, and if not from experience, then from the thousands of fight clips on YouTube. Out of all those fights caught on camera, how many were finished by one of the participants attacking any of the vital points we have talked about here? I haven't seen a single example yet. That should tell you something.

And staying on the topic of hitting heads, let's talk further about this in the next chapter.

Chapter 12|Create Space or Close Distance?

Let me ask you this: During a physical altercation, is it better to close distance with your attacker or create space between you and them?

Your answer to that question will depend essentially on how you train for such situations. Some people train to close down an opponent when they are under attack so they can get to grappling range. Others train to create space between themselves and their attacker so they can strike more easily.

But which strategy is best? Which one will offer you the most advantage and give you the greatest chance of prevailing in an attack situation?

The purpose of this chapter is to answer that question by looking at the advantages and disadvantages of both strategies to see if one is better or wiser than the other.

Closing Distance with An Attacker

The main advantage to closing distance with your attacker is that you are taking away their ability to strike. Most people need space, as well as grounding and torque in order to fire of an effective strike. Closing distance will take those things away from your attacker, leaving them all but helpless.

Apparently most people don't know what to do when their space and ability to strike effectively has been taken away from them. But if you are the one closing the distance then you will know exactly what to do, which, according to some, is to start using quarter beat strikes in conjunction with "shredding" the other guy to overwhelm and incapacitate him, or to initiate some kind of takedown technique.

Tactically speaking, this seems like a sound approach until you consider a couple of important factors. The first one is that, by taking away your attacker's ability to strike effectively, you are also, by default, taking away your own ability to strike effectively. Yes it is possible to strike from that range, but not so effectively. Quarter beat striking seems fine in theory and in a training environment when your opponent is wearing a protective helmet, but against a fully adrenalized attacker? Do you really think a quarter beat palm strike or a close in elbow strike is enough to put someone down? I doubt it.

You only have to look to MMA to see why this is true. Often in cage fights you will see two guys clinch and begin to use short range punches and elbows on each other. These strikes might be painful, they may even cut the other guy (in the case of elbows), but I don't think I've ever seen anyone get knocked out or even go down due to being hit by these short range strikes. You could argue that MMA fighters are used to such punishment, but so are many street fighters and criminals, and when you add in alcohol and drugs to the mix, you have an attacker who isn't going to feel much pain, much less hit the floor after you rap his head a few times with your palm. So against a determined attacker (and what attacker isn't determined?) quarter beat striking is all but useless and will not only stir up an attacker's aggression even further, but will also give them time to recreate the space that you just took away from them.

Of course I realise that these strikes are done in combination with techniques like the infamous Shredder. But is the Shredder really that effective against a real, slavering, highly aggressive and determined attacker? Is it enough to completely stop an attacker? I'm not so sure.

Face rubbing and scratching an attacker's face would cause discomfort no doubt; I don't think it would be enough to stop someone, however. And remember, we are talking about a fully adrenalized attacker here, not some role playing participant in a training environment. There is a big, nay *massive*, difference.

But what about attacking the eyes? That's part of the Shredder strategy. For sure, attacking the eyes can be a good tactic, but not really in the way that the Shredder does it. The Shredder presents a superficial attack to the eyes and not much more. If you want to attack the eyes then you have to attack them right. Use the thumbs to properly gouge the eyes—to actually strike into them—not just scratch or press on them. That would be more effective than any amount of scratching or face rubbing.

The other elephant in the room here is that effective self-defence techniques are supposed to work for even a person of average attributes and abilities. Given that the Shredder relies upon a person getting their opponent to a chest to back position, how is a smaller person – say a 100lb woman – supposed to get a larger man into that position in the first place? Against a fully resisting opponent, this can prove difficult for even a skilled fighter. And to then go on to "shred" their larger attacker's face? It's just not going to happen, I'm afraid.

Back when I was bouncing I used to close people down a lot, but that's mainly because I wanted to control and restrain them, not hit them. Hitting them would have been much easier, believe me. Trying to get even a small person chest to back if they are really resisting you can prove very difficult unless you are significantly bigger and stronger than most, which I wasn't.

Which brings me to my next point. Getting in that close, things can turn messy very quickly. Not only are you yourself open to punches to the head from your attacker (they mightn't knock you out but they aren't going to be pleasant either), but also biting and gouging. You take away someone's ability to hit and they will resort to savagery out of pure instinct. A wrestling match will often ensue at this distance as well. An attacker will hold on to you and if you try to take them down you will often go down with them.

Bottom line is that, for a small person, closing distance with a bigger attacker is suicide for they would just be playing right into their attacker's hands.

The other stated tactical advantage of getting in so close is the "psychological invasiveness" of doing so. Most people get very uncomfortable when you invade their space and get in their face, so, psychologically speaking, they are now cowering and you are at an advantage because you are used to working within such confined spaces.

This is debatable as well. Some people may feel a sense of panic when someone is that close to them, but enough to significantly affect their determination to hurt you? I doubt that. More likely it would push them into savagery, which in my experience is what happens when you get that close to a psyched up attacker, they resort to biting, gouging and clawing out of instinct or a sense of panic. The last thing I want in a fight is to get bitten. It's happened to me before when I closed a guy and ended up on the ground with him. It wasn't a pleasant experience. Neither was the tetanus shot I got the next day.

Creating Space in an Attack

So now let's look at why I consider creating distance to be a better option in an attack than closing it.

As I've already stated, by creating space you are giving your attacker the advantage of being able to use their strikes at full capacity, this is true. But you also have the exact same advantage, which is what many distance closers seem to forget. It then becomes a question of who can capitalise on this advantage the most and in the quickest time.

If you know how to set someone up to strike them and you know how to strike properly, this isn't actually much of a problem. It is certainly an easier proposition than trying to manhandle your attacker and finish them with face rubbing, face scratching and quarter beat strikes that have next to no impact potential. Again, for a smaller person against a larger person, this would be even more preposterous.

Same goes with grappling and wrestling techniques. Aside from the damage you may receive trying to get in close enough to grab your attacker, it can prove very difficult to take down a determined opponent. The chances are high that you will also end up on the ground with them. Tactically speaking, this wouldn't be a good move.

The fact is that the best and most effective way to stop an attack is to stop the attacker. The most effective way to do that is to *hit them on the head*, either knocking them out or hitting them enough times that they go down, at the very least giving you the chance to escape the situation.

None of that is possible when you close distance. You can't knock someone out with the Shredder and if things go sideways and you end up in a grappling match, how much harder is it going to be to escape then? If you are a woman being attacked by a sexual predator, your attacker will have you right where they want you—in their grasp!

All else aside, let's not forget about the single biggest contributing factor here: that of real world evidence.

The tactic of striking an attacker to the head to affect a knockout and finish the fight has been a proven one since time immemorial. We've been finishing fights like this since we lived in caves. Even chimpanzees fight like this; they batter their adversaries into submission (or death). In the history of fighting, striking the head has been the single biggest cause of victory. As a tactic it's as high percentage as you can get.

Now consider the Shredder. It was conceived of within the last twenty years or so and within that time I have never heard of anyone even trying to use it in a fight, much less successfully. If it was really that effective then everyone would be using it, would they not? And it's not like no one knows about it either. Anyone who trains in self-defence knows about the Shredder. The only people who claim to have used it are those who just happen to also teach it. I say this not to cause an argument, but only to point out that, for all the marketing and claims of effectiveness, there is little or no evidence to support these claims.

The same goes for BJJ in self-defence situations—lots of talk but no proof.

Just because a few select people can make a tactic or technique work for them doesn't make that tactic or technique effective in a broader sense. We all have techniques that only seem to work for us as individuals, but that doesn't mean we should expect them to work for everyone else as well.

When it comes to self-defence, whatever techniques are taught need to be high percentage techniques in that they will have a high chance of working in most situations. Not only that, they also need to work for the average person, not just for someone with superior strength, size or skills.

As a final point, you might argue that this all just a matter of personal preference. Some like to close the gap; others like to create a gap. Some like to grapple or shred; others like to strike. That's fine, all things being equal. If you have similar attributes to your opponent (equal size, weight, skills) then that argument might wash. But how often is this actually the case? How many women are the same size and have the same strength as their male attackers?

Self Defense Solutions

Few if any, which is why specialist or low percentage techniques can't be relied upon to get you out of trouble. To stand the greatest chance of getting out of trouble you need to use techniques and tactics that have been proven to work over and over again, not techniques that have no proof to validate them.

You feel annoyed after reading this. That's okay. It isn't my intention here to cause upset; I'm just dealing with the facts as they relate to self-defence. If someone can come along and prove to me different, then I'll happily listen.

Chapter 13|Force Disparity and Control and Restraint

Force disparity is a very useful concept that was introduced to me by another combatives instructor. Force disparity occurs when the level of force between you and your attacker is disproportionate. So if you try to respond to a high level of force with a lower level of force there will be a force disparity and your response will be too inadequate to stop your attacker, who is using a higher level of force.

This force disparity also applies when a small woman, for instance, is being attacked by a significantly larger man, or when you are faced by an aggressor with a weapon like a knife or a gun. The point is that there exists a reality at play here that many in the self-defence game don't want to admit exists. In some situations, where the odds are significantly stacked against you, the chances of you prevailing are slim to none, no matter how good your response to the situation is. In this context, many people out there who train in self-defence tend to suffer a bout of reality dyslexia and get to thinking that they can still prevail in circumstances where significant force disparity exists.

Where I find this concept most useful, however, is when you think about situations that involve family or friends. Over the years I have been unlucky enough to be involved in more than a few situations where close family or friends have kicked off at a social event and I have had the displeasure of trying to sort the situation out.

No doubt you have been in similar situations yourself. Perhaps you've had to witness a close relative at a family gathering drink too much and suddenly decide that anyone who comes within two feet of them is going to get hit. It doesn't matter what anyone else there does to try and calm the person down; the enraged and very drunk relative now sees everyone there as their enemy and has no qualms about hurting anyone who tries to calm them or restrain them.

The first couple of times I was involved in such a situation I tried to slip into bouncer mode and restrain the person who was causing all the trouble. Was I able to nicely restrain the person and calm them down? Hell no! What I got for my trouble was smacked in the face! Eventually I was able to take the other person down, but have you ever tried to hold someone down who doesn't want to be held down, and on top of that, is possessed of more strength than usual thanks to alcohol and adrenaline and red mist (rage)?

It isn't easy and you holding them down does nothing to calm them; it just makes them more enraged. Eventually you will have no choice but to let them back up, at which point they will kick off again and attack whoever is in their immediate vicinity, or they will seek out the person who they perceived to piss them off in the first place and try to attack them.

It's easy to see how these types of situations can get quickly out of control. I also find that, when family and friends are involved in such altercations, emotions tend to be higher since everyone knows each other so well. We tend to reserve the most rage for the ones we love.

The general consensus amongst martial artists and self-defence practitioners is that control and restraint is the only option in such volatile situations, and this consensus remains for two main reasons.

Firstly, it is thought that family and friends should be treated with respect and not hit. We'll discuss this in a moment. Secondly, it is thought that because someone is trained in martial arts they should be able to control anyone without hitting them. Both of these viewpoints are ridiculous in my opinion and only serve to show the lack of experience of those who spout this naïve nonsense.

Let's take that first point that family and friends should not be hit and should instead be restrained. Aside from the difficulty of restraining people who don't want to be restrained (which I'll discuss shortly), let's examine the circumstances that usually surround these kinds of situations.

Generally, when relatives or friends decide to kick off it is in a social setting, usually surrounded by a gathering of other family members and friends. When Uncle Jack suddenly flies into a rage and starts to fight with someone or everyone he is immediately putting everyone else in danger. In my experience, anyone who gets too close to a person who is enraged and under the influence is putting themselves in harm's way. They are going to get hit or worse. Plus, innocent bystanders may take damage in the process as those fighting may fall into them or worse. Anything could happen, and often does happen.

Now here's the thing. Uncle Jack, in deciding to kick off, has, in my opinion, relinquished any right he has to be treated softly or even with any respect. Knowingly or unknowingly, he has put everyone else in danger by his actions and he needs to be dealt with in whatever way possible. If he is hitting anyone who gets too close to him or endangering people in some other way, he has lost the right to be treated with kid gloves. The only priority now should be to stop him from endangering everyone else and that should be done in the quickest and most efficient way possible, without further endangering anyone else. If that means knocking Uncle Jack out, then so be it.

That second point — that martial artists should be able to restrain anyone — is also rubbish. Having spent a good number of years working doors I know how difficult it can be to restrain even the smallest of people if they don't want to be restrained. And let's be honest, who *does* want to be restrained? No one likes being manhandled and they will resist with all their might most of the time. There is also the force disparity issue that I mentioned at the start of this chapter. You will be trying to use a low level of force against someone who is using a much higher level of force, which is where the disparity comes in. That just isn't going to work. To have any hope of prevailing against someone who is using a high level of force, you must match that force.

I'm not saying control and restraint doesn't work, but it takes a certain amount of skill and experience to pull it off and it always helps if you are bigger and stronger than the person you are trying to restrain; the other way around doesn't work very well. Restraint is best done as a group, by multiple people swarming in and surrounding the person. That kind of team work is very effective. But are you really going to see that kind of team work at your average social gathering when probably no one else there knows what they are doing?

And what if you do manage to restrain Uncle Jack? Does that mean he will instantly calm down and stop struggling? In my experience, no, he won't. He will become even more enraged. People who have adrenalized themselves into high levels of aggression find it very difficult to come down from that. I remember a fight that kicked off between two of my close family members and I spent a full hour trying to restrain them both because I didn't want to hit them at the time. I had no help. As soon as I restrained one, the other would rush in and try to kick the person as I held them. This went back and forth for, as I say, a good hour. It only calmed down when one of the offending family members left the scene. That was a lesson learned for me.

What is that lesson? That in the situations described, the only good control and restraint is unconsciousness. That may sound macho or callous to you, but until you have been in one of these situations you will not understand. The quickest way to sort these people out when they kick off and the quickest way to prevent them putting others in danger is to hit them or choke them out. There will be no force disparity anymore. The situation can be ended quickly – and, hopefully, cleanly – and no one else can potentially get hurt.

Force disparity is certainly a concept you should keep in mind, for it will help to define your approach to certain situations. Even when you are training, it can help to consider the kinds of situations you might be using your techniques in.

An example of that would be when you are training highline strikes. As much as I like palm strikes, and as effective as they are, there are some situations where I wouldn't consider using them if a significant degree of force disparity existed. For instance, if I found myself facing a larger opponent who looked like they might do a lot of damage given the opportunity, I would choose to strike with my fists from the outset if a violent response was needed. Punches do more damage than palm strikes and damage is what is needed against a significantly larger or stronger or more capable opponent. I have more confidence in my fists than in my palms when all is said and done. So when I train my punches, I do so with those kinds of situations in mind. This helps to focus me as I practice.

The same goes for a situation where multiple opponents exist, or if an attacker has a weapon of some sort like a knife. Those odds represent a significant force disparity and whatever your response is, it has to be high up on the force continuum.

To put it in more blunt terms: In situations where a large degree of force disparity exists, you can't afford to mess about. You have to go in hard and fast and stay on the offensive or you will get beaten. It's as simple as that.

I also imagine that the force disparity concept might be a useful one to pull out in court should you find yourself in a position where you had to justify your actions in a certain situation. I'm not sure what difference this would make to your case, but I've no doubt that if you can articulate your actions in those terms—and as long as your actions where indeed justified in the first place—it certainly wouldn't harm your defence.

Chapter 14|Self Defence Psychology And Mental Training

In the self defence world much has been made of the "psychology" behind self defence itself. Ask many instructors what they think is most important when it comes to self defence and there answer (after awareness) will likely be the psychology of it all, or having the mental skills to be able to deal with and use violence when necessary.

While there is some truth behind this, in the main, the psychological aspects of self defence are vastly over-emphasised. It's an area that allows for the indulgence of all manner of theories and "head-work" techniques that at the end of the day, can't be shown to have any real value as far as teaching people how to protect themselves.

None of it can be proved because it exists only on the mental plain. Indeed the many theories and hypothesises that exist concerning self defence psychology, for the most part can't be proved to have any affect in the real world. So we are expected to take the word of the people who put this stuff out there.

There is no doubt it makes for interesting reading at times, but that's about it. I've yet to come across any psychological theory pertaining to self defence that could be said to be anyway useful to the average person who wants to get better at handling violent conflict.

The problem with most of the psychology stuff is that it is based on subjective experience and therefore can't be objectively evaluated. There are no studies to back anything up, only anecdotal evidence backed up by the often dubious authority of the person putting the stuff out there.

I have tried to put across the psychological aspects of self defence myself in the past (read my first book) but I have always made it clear that it is just my subjective opinion on things. It is okay to put across your own experiences so people may learn what they can from those experiences, but to put those experiences across as if they should apply to everyone would be wrong and not very scientific or objective.

Much of what passes for self defence psychology is the result of research porn. What happens is that a person gets really into a certain subject like self defence and they let their whims and indulgences carry them off to places that there is just no need to go. For instance, just because you study self defence doesn't mean you also have to make an in-depth study of the criminal mind by exploring criminology and sociology. When the chips are down, what possible use could such information have? None, I'm sure.

The same applies to "violence dynamics". Again there is this apparent need to "understand the enemy". From a pre-contact point of view I can see why some people feel there is a need for this sort of classification. Some attackers may have to be handled differently, but common sense and intuition should alert you to this anyway. Classifying attackers based on their motives complicates things more than is needed.

I can't really get behind the notion that the enemy must be studied and classified like animals in a lab. The only "enemy" that exists out there are people, and to a very large degree—on a base level— people are all the same.

Sure we all have different personalities, different attributes etc. But does this really matter when it comes to defending yourself against violence from another?

There are thousands of books and studies and research papers out there that seek to study and classify people who use criminal and violent behaviour to get their own way. And while some of this research is certainly interesting, do I really need to know every nuance of the average criminal mind? Do I need to know what motivates your average thug? Will knowing what motivates an attack on my person help me stop it? Professional law enforcement groups don't even delve that deep when they train people, and these are guys who deal with criminals day in and day out.

The fact is, if I'm being attacked by someone, I don't really care what is motivating their attack. All I know is that I'm being attacked and I need to defend myself—that's it, the bottom line. The psychology of my attacker matters not.

Why violence is perpetrated is much less important than *how* it is perpetrated, at least in self defence terms. It seems that we all have to know exactly what group a violent individual belongs to now; we have to know the motivation behind their particular brand of violence. Are they Monkey Dancers, Status Seekers, Resource or

Process Predators? So many different classifications for what amounts to essentially the same thing: a violent cunt!

In the case of predators, I don't care if they want my money or my head in their fridge. My response will be the same if I am physically threatened. I will fight back.

Sure, if someone threatens me with a knife and demands my wallet, I'll give them the damn thing. That's just common sense. That's being socially intelligent and understanding the type of situation I am in and how it can be resolved.

I've been a member of society long enough now. I don't need academic classifications to help me function around people or in society in general.

Teaching violence dynamics is a bit like teaching awareness, in that you are trying to make academic what is already intuitively felt. With awareness, you are either switched on or you aren't. With violence dynamics, either you know people or you don't.

Reading about people and hearing someone else talk about people is not going to help you deal with them any better. I could read books all day long about life in prison and the culture that exists in prison and how people act in prison. Does this mean that if I end up in prison that I'll be able to expertly classify and handle every person in there? Of course not. The only way I'd survive in prison is by getting to know the place and its inhabitants first hand, not by reading a book on it.

It's all very interesting this criminal psychology stuff, but in the end, most of it is no more than research porn—pointless reams of data that only serve to complicate the issue at hand.

What so-called interpersonal violence comes down to is that there is someone in front of you that wants to hurt you. The circumstances surrounding this should be obvious to anyone with half a brain. If someone demands my money or car then I know what they want. If someone jumps me in a dark alley then I know what they want. If some dick in a bar tries to pick a fight with me then I know what they want. In each case, I will respond accordingly, using my intuition and common sense.

Whether you face a mugger, a serial killer or some weekend warrior, in the grand scheme of things, it doesn't matter. Your response will be the same in that you will do whatever it takes to stop that other person from hurting you, no matter what their motivations are.

At the end of the day, what is going to help you most in a self defence situation is not what you know about the psychology of your attacker, but the training you have done to learn how to stop him.

It is proper training that will give you the tools you need to protect yourself in a self defence situation. Even if you are lacking in confidence or are struggling with the fear side of things, good combatives training will help you overcome those limitations.

You must also remember that we are all individuals with our own particular strengths and weaknesses. Training of any kind does not guarantee the same results for everyone. Combatives will not help you fix every personal issue that you have, nor is it guaranteed to make you into this confident, highly assertive person who is capable of handling any self defence situation.

Often you will have to take the bull by the horns and work on your personal problems outside of training. Combatives isn't some cure all. It is designed to teach people how to use certain tools and tactics in particular situations. It does not offer magical solutions to all your problems.

I can tell you what it is that I do to make myself mentally stronger, or I can tell you about some of the mental processes I might use to help me handle difficult situations better, but that doesn't mean those things will work for you. You have to find your own way of dealing with things. Sorry if that doesn't equate with some of the solutions and shortcuts offered by some, but that is the reality.

People are desperate for these quick fix solutions to their problems. They say they shit themselves when faced by an attacker and ask how they can overcome their fear. You don't! The reality is, almost everyone shits themselves when faced by someone who wants to hurt them. That's life. This is something you must learn to accept instead of agonising over solutions that don't exist. There is nothing out there that will make a person fearless, except snake oil. The only solution to that particular problem is to try and harden yourself to the feelings associated with conflict, and you can do that through training. Training will help certainly, but training can only do so much. That's just something you have to accept.

My advice (and I'm speaking from experience here) is to forget about trying to find quick fixes and easy solutions to complex problems. Quit drinking the snake oil. Concentrate instead on your training and work hard to get results from it. Over time you will get most of what you need just from training. The rest you will have to find for yourself. It is naive to think that everything will be handed to you on a plate.

While we are on the subject of training and mental skills, let me end this chapter by talking about yet more snake oil that people can't help drinking.

At one point I spent months researching so-called "mental toughness" and "mental training" techniques because I planned to write a book on the subject as it related to self defence. I read numerous books, articles and research papers on the subject of raising your game by improving your mental game.

When I started the research I felt sure that it would be possible to take my training (and that of others) to the next level. This belief was based not only on my intuition that mental training alongside physical training made complete sense, but also on the fact that so many high profile athletes talked a lot about the importance of the mental game and how "90% of their game was mental".

Well after all that research, what I found was that so-called mental training techniques are mostly bullshit. In the main, what passes for mental training techniques are actually just NLP (Neuro Linguistic Programming) inspired nonsense and have little or no value at all when it comes to raising your game.

The whole field of sports psychology in fact appears to be based on a lot of bullshit pop psychology and shaky research. Despite the claims made by those who call themselves sports psychologists, the techniques and practices that are used in this field to try and raise the mental game of athletes appear to make very little difference to an athlete's performance at the end of the day.

This is none more true than when it comes to applying this stuff to self defence, and also to law enforcement and the military. There is a lot of anecdotal evidence to suggest that it makes a difference, but little in the way of any concrete evidence to prove that it does.

With any study conducted, there is always going to be "evidence" that is biased towards proving the validity of the study itself. You only have to look at the mountains of research done on human paranormal abilities. Many studies claim to have proved the existence of such abilities and there is much anecdotal evidence to suggest that they have, but amongst all that evidence there is still no concrete proof that human paranormal abilities even exist.

I found the same sort of thing with mental toughness techniques and mental training techniques. Any evidence is based solely on subjective hearsay and not much else. The sports psychology field seems to be no different from the NLP field in that it is populated by pseudo-scientists and confidence tricksters, telling people what they want to hear and backing up there outrageous claims with dubious science and shaky psychology.

Certain aspects of the mental game can be improved upon—I'm not saying this isn't possible. Techniques like visualisation are useful, as is learning to concentrate and focus better, and learning to stay calm under pressure. With a bit of conscious effort, these things can be improved.

In the main though, mental toughness and learning to control your mental game can only come through playing the damn game all the time and gathering as much experience as possible. The more you play and practice the better you will get at controlling your own mind. It's as simple as that.

But that isn't enough for some. It wasn't enough for me when I started my research. I had visions of designing a complete program of mental skills training to run alongside the physical programs. Then I saw what was actually on most these mental programs.

All of the mental training programs that I studied where made up of what can only be described as self-indulgent rubbish. These programs where made by people who were desperate to justify the need for such programs, and also to justify the role they themselves were playing, the role of sports psychologist or mental training coach or whatever title they went under.

Almost all of the techniques in these programs where based around NLP concepts, which in itself should be cause for concern because NLP is nothing more than bullshit packaged up as cutting edge science and "neuropsychology". It has no scientific basis and it is propagated by confidence tricksters who like to prey on the weak-minded.

So to base an entire field of psychology on this nonsense? Hardly a base for credibility is it?

The fact is people at the top of their fields get there because they work hard and they work smart. They understand everything there is to know about what it is they do, and they practice the hell out of every part of their game. They are also experienced players who learn from every game. They already know how to get the most from themselves, they don't need a load of silly mental training techniques to increase their confidence or help them do better.

They get that from training and applying themselves in whatever way they need too so they can get results.

In the end, either you have game or you don't. No amount of bullshit psychology or mental training techniques are going to change that.

For self defence it's no different. If you can't get what you need from training or from your own experience then you will never get it.

Your time will be far better spent by being consistent with the fundamentals. Every master of their field works this way. They spend their time doing the things that will have the greatest impact on their performance and development.

Avoid the snake oil. It will just poison you eventually.

Chapter 15|Taking Your Time

I'd like to end this book by talking about something that is very rarely mentioned in relation to self-defence – even though it is vitally important to getting good results – and that is the value of taking your time.

Once upon a time people used to serve apprenticeships. They would spend five to ten years learning some kind of trade from a master tradesman. The goal of such a long apprenticeship was so the apprentice could master every skill involved in their trade and eventually become a master tradesman just like their mentor. To get to that level of mastery though, the apprentice had to put in many thousands of hours of practice, showing complete commitment and dedication to what they were doing.

That level of commitment and desire for mastery still exists to some extent today in society, but I am not sure that it exists in the self-defence industry so much. Usually when someone talks about learning self-defence they talk about learning it in a matter of weeks or months at the most, sometimes even *days*. There are organisations out there who promise to make anyone an instructor in self-defence in just two or three days! That is obviously marketing and greed gone too far, but it characterises the general view in the industry that self-defence can be learned by anyone almost overnight.

Clearly this viewpoint is nonsense. While it may be possible to teach people a few basic techniques over the course of a few weeks—techniques that they *may* be able to put to use if it came to it—it is certainly not possible to train someone to a high level of competence in self-defence, nor indeed qualify them as an instructor.

If it is your goal to become highly competent in combatives and fighting in general, then you are looking at five to ten years' training at least. The thought of committing themselves for so long would no doubt horrify a lot of people, which is why so many go for the quick fix and walk around afterwards kidding themselves that they know what they are doing when it comes to fighting and self-defence.

I am a big believer that if you are going to do something then you do it right. Commit to whatever it is you are doing and make your goal nothing less than mastery.

Otherwise, what is the point in doing it at all? Why do something if all you are going to be is mediocre at it? Mediocrity in all its forms should be deeply offensive to you. Why? Because being mediocre at something means that you could be better if you worked at it more. It tells people that you are not committed enough to be any better; that you are just passing time without expending too much effort.

Don't go for "just alright". Strive for awesome!

If you are training in combatives then I assume that you are expecting good results from your training, otherwise why do it in the first place, right? So how much time and effort are you putting in to getting those results? Are you in it for the long haul? How do you feel about putting in five to ten years of solid training and study? These are questions you should ask yourself. If the idea of committing yourself to such an extent is too much for you, then perhaps you should find something else to do where you *can* commit yourself to that extent because you are not going to get anywhere near results if you don't.

Getting good results from your training is largely based on your ability to take your time and not rush the process. Obviously the type of training you do matters as well, but assuming everything else is in place, taking your time will ensure you get the results you are after.

And remember we are talking about mastery here. We are talking about knowing your subject inside and out, in great detail; we are talking about having superior physical abilities and intuition. Those things take time to develop.

Taking Your Time in Training

If you have ever been in a fight then you will know what a panic move is. It's one of those moves that you do without thinking, in a panicked state. Nearly always these kinds of moves turn out to be very ineffectual. An example of a common panic move is to lash out unthinkingly in the general direction of your opponent as you try to land a strike on them. Invariably, the strike will have little power and the accuracy will be way off. In fact you'll probably miss your target completely due to the fact that you didn't really focus on a target—you merely blindly lashed out hoping to hit something.

Another example of a panic move would be if you were taking a lot of hits from your opponent and you blindly rushed forward in a panic to close distance and grab hold of your attacker, half hoping that this will end the punishment they are dealing out to you. Now you would find yourself in a wrestling match, probably still getting hit. The fight would go to the ground and more panic moves would follow.

I remember going to the ground with a guy one time and, in a panic, I gripped his throat and held it. I didn't do anything else; I just held it, even though there were plenty of other targets open to me for striking. I stayed that way for what seemed like a long time before waking up and getting back to my feet. That was a panic move—pointless and fairly ineffectual as it turned out.

These kinds of panic moves are understandable under the pressure of a real fight. None of us are so experienced that nothing fazes us or we never get surprised by things that happen in the fight. It is natural to blindly react and lash out at times under those kinds of circumstances. And to be honest, that's the way it will always be when the shit hits the fan. To what degree this occurs will depend on your training and level of experience in such situations.

Panic moves under real circumstances are forgivable. Where they are *not* too forgivable is in training. I have observed in many of the students I have worked with, especially at the beginning of their training, the tendency to default to panic moves when they are under even the smallest amount of pressure.

As an example, I might ask a trainee to perform a highline strike on the pad and then follow that strike up with three more. Invariably the first strike will be fine but the three follow up strikes will be rushed, performed in a panic and consequently far from adequate in terms of power and effectiveness. The trainee sometimes nearly trips over himself in an effort to quickly do those three strikes. The dead give-away is when the student slaps at the pad instead of striking it if they are doing a palm strike. This is nearly always an indication that the student is in panic mode, which comes from not being centred enough as they strike.

If this habit of falling into panic mode is not soon corrected it will become instilled in the student and they will find it hard to break the habit. As time goes on and the student is put under increasing pressure through various drills, the panic moves will become more and more of a hindrance to their overall performance and they will not achieve the results they desire from their training.

The Antidote to Panic Moves

So what is the antidote to panic moves? The solution is to make your moves assured. You want to be doing assured moves instead of panic moves. The terminology might not have the best ring to it, but it nonetheless sums up what I'm trying to get at when I say that your moves should be assured.

Assured movements are controlled, focused and powerful—the opposite of what a panic move is. Acquiring this kind of assuredness in your movements requires that you learn to take your time when performing techniques, as much as possible anyway under whatever circumstances you are in. Obviously, the more pressure you are under, the harder this will be.

To make your moves more assured, and to avoid falling into a panic every time you have to hit the accelerator, so to speak, you will have to learn to take your time with things. This means you will have to learn how to focus and also centre yourself. It will involve reigning yourself in and not letting your mind take control of your body. If your mind thinks there is a panic to get something done then your body will soon concur, which results in the panic moves we talked about.

Making your strikes and overall movements more assured is a simple process. Purposely relax and tell yourself that you will not rush and that you have plenty of time to complete the given task. By doing this *you* are taking control of your mind first of all and telling it that you are in control. Focus and breathe easy. Get a calm centre. Make sure that your mind is detached from the outcome you want to achieve. If you allow your mind to focus too much on the outcome your mind will think there is a lot at stake and panic won't be too far away. Just be confident and assured and know that you have the ability to do what you have to do. Then simply do your strikes on the pad. You should find yourself taking your time more, which will result in more effective striking.

This is very simple. I don't want to make it seem like there is some complicated mental process involved. There isn't. It's just a matter of checking yourself to make sure you are centred before you do what you have to do. That's it. That's usually all it takes. You just need to do this every time before you do your drills.

Start with the simple drills to get used to the process. It should become instilled after a time and eventually carry over into the more pressurised drills where you won't have as much time (or any time) to consciously focus. This is why the habit of getting centred and focusing needs to become subconscious and automatic. The only way to ensure this is to practice, and to cultivate the habit of making your movements as assured as possible.

Keeping a Level Head

Try to take a Zen-like approach to your training. Don't invest too heavily in outcomes; focus more on the process. Investing too heavily in outcomes will lead to needless pressure and disappointment when you don't perform the way you would like. Keep a balanced mind. Nothing that happens in training –good or bad – should illicit in you any kind of high emotion. Keep yourself in check always, whether you make a big mistake or whether you do something great. Either way, don't make a big deal out of it because it probably isn't.

Keeping yourself in check in this way, keeping the panic moves to a minimum and the assured moves to a maximum, will greatly improve the results you get from your training. You are controlling that instinctive need to panic and cultivating a sense of assuredness in everything that you do. It's a conscious growth process.

Of course, the more pressure that you find yourself under, the harder all this will be. Don't despair when you fall apart sometimes and resort to panic moves. Sometimes, if the pressure is great enough, this is all that we can do. Accept that it happened and resolve to do your best to prevent it from happening again.

One of the goals of hard skills training is to effectively make someone into a machine who does precise machine-like movements. That's fair enough. Remember, though, that we are also human and as such can be infallible at times, prone to failure and mistakes. Don't let this aspect of human nature get to you. Accept it and strive to get better at minimizing it.

Neal Martin

Afterward

I hope you enjoyed reading this book. Like I said in the beginning, my purpose in writing the book was to get you to think about your approach to your training and to consider whether or not you are getting the results you desire from that training. If those results fall short, applying the things I talked about in this book will definitely improve them.

The real trick to getting desirable results is to become more conscious about what you are doing. You need to make yourself aware of the real issues involved in self defence training and the purpose behind the things you do in it.

If you have no clear idea of why you are training or of the kinds of situations you are training *for* and the problems involved, you will not be able to come up with suitable answers to those problems. You'll be groping blindly in the dark.

This is why it is very important to gather as much information and experience as possible, and to learn as much as possible from others who are more experienced than you. If you can train under the right people, your game will improve considerably.

Combatives isn't just about copying what others are doing though. To get the greatest level of understanding and competence you have to think for yourself as well. Knowing things on a surface level isn't enough if you want to attain any level of mastery.

The kind of understanding I am talking about takes time however and you must be patient and prepared for that. Your patience and dedication will pay off though when you reach the point of really knowing your stuff and of having a clear understanding of the issues involved in training and the kind of solutions that are required to resolve those issues.

You will always be learning of course. As much as I know now, there is still a lot that I don't know yet. That's the process though. That's what the journey is all about.

Train hard.

Train honest.

Question everything.

Neal Martin

Think for yourself.

And don't forget to have fun along the way.

Neal

Other Books By Neal Martin

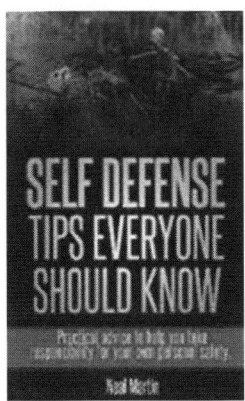

Self Defense Tips Everyone Should Know

Self defense tips based on what works in the real world.

The most no-bullshit self defense book you will ever read.

Reviews:

"...a book extrapolated from real world experience that is based on reality and not academic theory."

"...what you read here could very well save your life someday."

"...the ONLY book I've read that has given me any real confidence in my ability to defend myself properly. GET IT."

In this book you will learn:

- How to properly take responsibility for your personal safety
- How to formulate a self defense game-plan that works
- How to sharpen your awareness skills and stay "switched on"
- How to conquer fear and adrenaline
- How to really hit hard and hit first when necessary
- The self defense techniques that instil panic in your attacker and force them to capitulate
- And much more

By the time you finish reading this book you will have a complete self defense game-plan in place. You will know more about how to protect yourself than most people out there, even the ones who train in self defense already!

Self Defense Solutions

Combatives Instruction

A book for all instructors and students of self defence who strive for excellence in their teaching and training.

Reviews:

"...like Hemingway on fighting." B. Williams

"...an accurate treatise on the Western World view of effective strategy and tactics" The Shrike

"...one of the best books I have read on self defense." Geordie Henderson

A completely practical guide on self defense training methods that will give you:

- A complete blueprint for teaching and training combatives

- A detailed and fully explained combatives syllabus for you to work from
- Essential training practices and guidelines
- The best self defense techniques to teach and train
- Numerous example training drills
- Guidelines for developing your students (and yourself)
- And much more

This book details all the essential elements of teaching combatives the right way so that you can get the results you and your students are looking for.

About The Author

Neal Martin is a writer and a martial artist with over thirty years training experience. His speciality is combatives and self defence. Neal lives in N.Ireland with his wife and daughters.

Contact via email: neal.martin@hotmail.com

Contact via Facebook: www.facebook.com/CombativeMind

Website: www.combativemind.com

Printed in Great Britain
by Amazon.co.uk, Ltd.,
Marston Gate.